A SHORT HISTORY OF THE
AMERICAN LABOR MOVEMENT

A SHORT HISTORY
OF THE
AMERICAN LABOR
MOVEMENT

BY

MARY BEARD

GREENWOOD PRESS, PUBLISHERS
NEW YORK   1968

PREFACE

91457

This little book is intended as a brief and simple story of the labor movement in the United States from the day of independence to the present time. Although there are many special studies, there is no single, comprehensive volume of moderate size for the busy citizen. It seems hardly necessary to dwell upon the importance of more exact and more widespread knowledge of the history, aims and methods of labor organizations in this country.

This volume is largely based upon the monumental *History of Labor in the United States* by John R. Commons, David J. Saposs, Helen L. Sumner, E. B. Mittelman, H. E. Hoagland, John B. Andrews, and Selig Perlman. Several other books, however, have been used with the aforesaid text, especially for the history since 1905. Among these supplementary books may be mentioned: P. F. Brissenden, *The I. W. W.: a Study in American Syndicalism* (Columbia University Studies); M. Hillquit, *History of Socialism in the United States; Reports of Proceedings of the Annual Conventions of the American Federation of Labor;* Stanwood, *History of the Presidency* (Vols. I and II) for all party platforms;

v

F. Engels, *Socialism: Utopian and Scientific;* C. Becker, *History of Political Parties in the Province of New York;* Alice Henry, *The Trade Union Woman;* Edith Abbott, *Woman in Industry;* and the writings of Samuel Gompers. Florence Thorne has given invaluable critical aid.

MARY RITTER BEARD.

CONTENTS

A SHORT HISTORY OF THE
AMERICAN LABOR MOVEMENT

A SHORT HISTORY OF THE AMERICAN LABOR MOVEMENT

CHAPTER I

NATURE AND SIGNIFICANCE OF THE LABOR MOVEMENT

Labor movement—definition.—Every modern industrial country has a labor movement; that is, an organized and continuous effort on the part of wage earners to improve their standards of living over a national area. The outward and visible signs of this movement are trade unions, national federations, strikes, boycotts, lockouts, labor leaders, labor conferences and programs, injunctions, legal battles, prosecutions, co-operative societies, labor and socialist parties, a labor press and labor propaganda, the participation of labor in partisan politics, labor lobbies in legislatures, and labor colleges and educational experiments. Considered as a state of mind, the labor movement is marked by growing sympathy among all crafts, trades, and classes of workers—

1

an increasing belief that their cause is, at bottom, one cause.

Origin of the American movement.—The American labor movement began in self-defense—in attempts of workers to protect themselves against the ravages of the rising industrial system as it proceeded step by step to transform the simple agricultural society of the eighteenth century into the urban and industrial society of the nineteenth century. Attempts to trace modern labor organization back to the guilds of the middle ages have been vain. Not until the rise of the merchant capitalist, the factory system, the growth of great industrial cities, mining, and transportation on a large scale did the modern working-class movement emerge.

Peculiarities of the American labor movement.—While they have the same origin, the labor movements of the various modern nations differ in their membership, structure, policies and leadership. The American movement has had a distinct character on account of the peculiar political and economic conditions prevailing in this country. Although in early times we had a great planting aristocracy in the southern states, and a landed aristocracy in New York, feudalism never got a strong hold in America.

There never was a powerful landed nobility and clergy to dispute the growing power of the *bourgeoisie* and labor. Our national history therefore had a more purely economic coloring from the start.

The independence of our nation originated in a trade and taxation dispute and in that dispute mechanics and artisans were keenly interested. They played a vigorous rôle in organizing opposition to British rule, in formulating revolutionary policies, and in waging war against royal armies on American soil.* Although there were, at first, property qualifications on the right to vote, the suffrage was more widely extended than in England; and early in the nineteenth century the workingmen of the northern states were given the ballot without their having to wage a savage struggle against the ruling classes, such as was carried on in Europe.

Many other forces gave a particular trend to the American labor movement. For more than a hundred years there was an abundance of cheap land in the West so that any laborer, with a little capital and some enterprise, who was discontented with his lot as an industrial worker, could readily become an independent farmer. Then the American workers have had to bargain over an immense market area, with extraordinary opportunities for speculation and personal gain. They have had to compete with an enormous and continuous stream of unorganized immigrants from all parts of the world. They have been compelled to carry on their work of organization in every known tongue and to surmount the

* Becker, History of Political Parties in the Province of New York (University of Wisconsin Studies).

almost insuperable obstacles of race prejudices, different languages, alien habits. They have been compelled to battle with gigantic business organizations known as trusts and combinations, commanding billions of dollars and monopolizing markets on a national scale. No industrial workers have had to face fiercer competition, a mightier money power, more temptations to desert the labor movement, and a heavier loss of leaders to politics and other causes. Finally, it may be noted that the long and terrible struggle over negro slavery, which occupied the political arena for more than thirty years and culminated in a fratricidal war of four years' duration, seriously checked the early labor movement and kept it many decades behind the movement in England. It was not until free land was nearly all gone in the early nineties and that avenue of escape closed to workmen that the American labor movement assumed the solidarity that characterizes the movement in other countries.

The universality of the labor movement.—In spite of national peculiarities the labor movement has overleaped national boundaries. Economic conditions are swiftly becoming the same the world over. The steam engine and railway are making all nations industrial and, wherever mechanical industry appears on a large scale, there appears also a labor movement. As trade becomes international and the market a world market, the labor leaders in the several countries tend to draw together to exchange ideas, work out programs for common action, and protect the workers of each country against the competition of other countries.

International conferences of organized workers have been held at fairly regular intervals since 1864. The American labor movement was drawn into international relations five years later when it sent its first delegate to Basle in the hope that some way might be found to stem the tide of cheap immigrant labor pouring into this country, lowering the wage scale and thereby the standard of living for American workers. Such a powerful factor in the field of international relations had labor movements become in 1919 that the Peace of Versailles provided for an official international labor conference in an effort to equalize and stabilize working conditions throughout the world. The first of these official world labor conferences, composed of men selected by their respective governments, met in Washington, in October, 1919. Thus the strongest governments take cognizance of the international character of labor relations, forced upon the attention of the world by the efforts of organized labor.

Significance of the labor movement.—For a long time this wide-spread labor movement was almost entirely ignored by everybody save those who took part in it or were in sympathy with it or at least intellectually curious about it. Members of the professional classes, for the most part, thought of it only in times of crisis. It is a significant comment on American intellectuals that it was not until 1918 that there was any authoritative and exhaustive history of the American labor movement. It is still more significant that the preparation of this history was undertaken, not by professional historians, but by economists who could not after all entirely ignore labor in studying industry.

There are, however, occasions when this extraordinary movement sharply engages the attention of the "public"—a term often used in America to indicate the great metropolitan newspapers. In a crisis like the Great War, the general public became suddenly aware that it could not ignore the attitude of organized labor toward the production of ships, munitions, army supplies, and fuel at a high rate of speed and without interruption by strikes and trade disputes. The prosecution of modern wars rests completely upon the operations of labor in mines, mills, and factories, so that labor fights there just as truly as the soldiers do in the trenches. No ships; no transportation of men and supplies. No clothing; a ragged and demoralized army. No munitions; no advance, no defense. Organized labor thus in fact holds the key to the fighting power of modern states. It not only influences, by its policies, the millions enrolled in its ranks; it actually holds in its grip the millions outside of its pale. In war times, therefore, it is watched with awe, tense and constant, as a mighty power—for good or ill, according to the opinion of the observer.

Again the labor movement is recognized as a factor in national affairs when it breaks out in disturbances or demonstrations of its power; such as, strikes, boycotts, or riots which make trouble for consumers, employers, the government, and the humanitarians. The United States has had its full share of such disturbances. They have been intensified by the violence of the industrial panics which have periodically deranged American business, spreading ruin and bankruptcy far and wide, and resulting in unemployment, misery, and starvation in labor circles.

Labor also arouses public interest when it turns aside from bargaining with employers to demand certain laws and policies at the hands of the politicians, or threatens to break into politics on its own account. At such times, it has to be considered, placated, or, to use the common term, "suppressed." The "labor vote" thus becomes a pawn in the political game or the object of derision on the part of those who seek applause by taking a "firm and uncompromising stand against paltering with class politics." From the days of Andrew Jackson to the present time, labor has been periodically "in politics." From time to time it has wrung from state legislatures and from Congress special concessions in the form of legislation; it has often declared its independence and elected labor members of boards of aldermen, legislatures and Congress.

The story of the labor movement is not, however, merely a record of spectacular events. Even the most dramatic outbreak—a political campaign, direct action, or violence—must be traced to its cause. It is an uninformed person who ascribes every crisis in American labor to sudden hysteria or alien ferment. Nor can outbreaks be considered apart from results. Sometimes distinct social gains flow from what seems to the outsider to be just aimless unrest; for example, that in 1910 which registered the rise of sweat shop workers in the garment trades from degrading conditions of life and labor.

Moreover, it is easy to magnify the stormy scenes in labor history. Historians make a grave mistake when they dwell solely on its turbulent features. Achievements gained by militancy often form the basis of constructive work in times of peace. The story of the movement cannot be told in head lines, but is a chronicle of steady and patient organization, moderate legislation, loyalty to thousands of contracts, prompt supply of skilled labor, standardization of practices, vast productiveness in industry, and unmistakable mental growth.

Naturally a movement of so many phases produces varied types of leaders—from the harsh and indomitable man of action to the shrewd and hard-headed organizer engaged in the humdrum work of daily

constructive effort. As labor grows more conscious
of its historic mission, it is inevitably thinking more
about the character of its leadership in all parts
of this country. To play a rôle in the state requires
statesmanship.

Finally the labor movement is more than an economic enterprise or a field for energetic leadership.
It has a deep social and spiritual significance. It
draws men and women together in a great coöperative undertaking which grows in strength day and
night and develops ideals of peace and well-being in
society as well as practical contests of force. The
form of labor's organization and its program change
from time to time but its numerical strength in-
creases and its growing solidarity gives more and
more weight to its counsels. Even though it may
always remain a minority movement in point of
membership among the workers, it will exercise the
power that a minority always exercises in proportion
to its clearness of purpose, its efficiency of organization, and the integrity of its directors. A mere
counting of heads is not the essence of democratic
achievement. Indeed the labor movement, with such
numbers as it gets, takes on the form of a great
social force akin to titanic forces in the natural
world. Anything so fundamental, so impressive,
so fraught with possibilities for the future surely
deserves an intensive study by those outside the labor
movement as well as by those who work within it.

CHAPTER II

ORIGIN OF AMERICAN TRADE UNIONS

Local labor organizations in colonial times.—
There were no trade unions in the modern sense in
the American colonies under British dominion.
There were labor organizations in the towns but they
were friendly and benevolent societies formed by
mechanics and journeymen. They were similar in
spirit to those formed among master employers.
Their main purpose was to take care of members in
times of illness or financial distress. They were
friendly societies in an age when public hospitals,
homes for the aged, poor farms, pensions, and charitable institutions were not sustained on a large
scale by public taxation. They were formed by the
new town-dwellers—printers, shoemakers, smiths,
and carpenters,—who had been separated from the
soil and therefore had no individual resources to fall
back upon in an emergency. Just as members of
the same church, race, or neighborhood drew together
for mutual aid, so the mechanics drew together to
help one another. As there were no banks or credit
societies, these early trade societies kept chests for

10

the deposit of money and, on occasion, loaned money to members in need.   In addition to their benevolent features, they acted as censors of the quality of the work of their members and even censored morals as well as workmanship.   When they were legally incorporated, it was with the express stipulation that they were not to interfere with wages, hours of labor, and similar economic matters.   In short, they were not trade unions as we understand that term to-day.

Independence opens a new era in industry and labor.—With American independence, an entirely new set of forces came into play.   Great Britain had supervised and restricted American enterprise in the interest of the mother country.   When her restraints were thrown off, Americans thought they could develop their own industries in their own way. They could trade with all countries of the world and thus widely extend their markets, increasing the demand for their goods.   Great Britain, being anxious to retain industries for herself, had sought to keep the colonies agricultural in character.   British control being broken, the Americans leaped with zeal into the industrial field.   They had an abundance of natural resources of all kinds, and they no longer had an outside force to stay their hands.

The adoption of the Constitution marks a commercial revolution.—The period that followed independence (1776) was one of war and weakness, but when the new form of government was established in

1789, giving strength to the union of states and
security to business, American enterprise was soon
manifest. Under the Constitution, a national bank
was founded to give a common medium of exchange
throughout the country; uniform currency was introduced; treaties with foreign powers were negotiated;
the tariffs which the states had formerly imposed on
goods coming from other states were broken down.
In a word, the American market was extended over
the entire United States. Commercial warfare between the states was stopped. Finances were put on
a sound basis. American credit abroad was established firmly and foreign capital to develop iron,
steel, ship building and other industries was secured
in abundance. With social order guaranteed, plenty
of capital at hand, unlimited natural resources, a
national market available, a world market opened, a
generous supply of European labor assured through
immigration, American business men could swing
forward with their industries on a large scale.

**The great market opened by the merchant capi-
talist.**—The great market was first opened by a
peculiar type of business man, the merchant capitalist. He was not usually the owner of industries nor
the employer of artisans. He was a trader and mid-
dle-man, mediating between the producer and the
consumer. He specialized in buying and selling. His
motto was: "Buy in the cheapest market and sell
in the dearest market." He therefore bought up

immense supplies, sometimes in Europe, and sometimes in Boston, Providence, Hartford, New York,
Philadelphia and wherever they could be found.
These he accumulated in warehouses at one or more
points and sold in large quantities to local store-
keepers, competing sharply with the local master and
his workman.

**The merchant capitalist conquers local em-
ployers.**—The community market was being sup-
planted by a national and even international market.
Now the cheapest market in which to buy was the
market in which production was the most advanced
and, as American industries were far behind those
of Europe, the merchant capitalist bought most of
his goods abroad.   Thus he incurred the odium of
American employers, employees, and patriots like
Washington and Hamilton who wanted to develop
home industries.   Americans who thought they
could capture the European market by being freed
from England found themselves captured instead by
traders in foreign goods.   The merchant capitalist
made steady headway, bringing under his thumb the
local employer whose community market he invaded,
undercutting him in the sale of goods.   The employer,
who in older and simpler days could take sides with
his workmen against the community in fixing wages
and prices, could no longer do this.   He lost his
monopoly over prices in his own market.   If he met

the competition of cheap goods from abroad, or from other American towns, he had to cut wages.

Employers and workmen seek protection.—The merchant capitalist thus found natural enemies in both American employers and workmen. Out of the struggle against him four important results ensued: (1) a national protective tariff policy; (2) attempts of masters and men to increase the quantity and improve the quality of their output; (3) the separation of the employees from their employers and the formation of unions designed to uphold wages; (4) the recognition by the workmen of themselves as a distinct group in the community with interests of their own in markets and wages to be sustained by the strength of organization against all comers.

At first as anxious as their employers to secure protection against cheap foreign goods brought in by the merchant capitalist, workmen supported the adoption of the new federal Constitution and approved the enactment of tariff laws laying duties on imports. They also combined with their master employers in associations to improve their respective trades and crafts. An Association of Mechanics and Manufacturers was formed in Providence in 1789 "for the purpose of promoting industry and giving a just encouragement to ingenuity." In Boston and Charleston, shipwrights and caulkers offered premiums for inventions and made every effort to spur the younger workers to use their minds in improving methods and tools. In Boston the printers employed chemists to perfect type, paper, ink and other products. A patent law passed in 1790 gave protection to American inventors. Apprentice schools and libraries were established in New York and Philadelphia with a view to increasing the skill and productiveness of workmen and masters. Every encouragement was given to young men to establish shops of their own in order that skill and independence might be blended in American labor in the future as in colonial times. Even loan funds were created, Benjamin Franklin leaving £1000 for this object because he had been established in the printing business in this manner. Thus labor and employers united in a common protection against the merchant capitalist who was invading American markets with cheap goods.

Labor breaks away from employers.—With all their efforts at self-protection and improvement in the technique of their industry, the industrial workers, however, saw a steady trend toward cheap wares and low wages. In all parts of the country, the merchant capitalist carried on his operations, buying and selling domestic products as well as disposing of his foreign stocks. Societies of master employers, which had been mainly benevolent, now changed to associations to keep down wages in order that they might secure contracts with the middleman, the merchant capitalist. Labor associations with benevolent purposes gave way to trade unions organized for protection against the invader who cut prices and wages and looked solely to profits. Labor also began to divorce itself from societies of manufacturers and master mechanics formed to train apprentices and improve methods of production. Workingmen began to say: "What is the use of improving our skill and increasing our output, if we cannot protect ourselves against falling wages?"

The rise of the trade union.—Such were the circumstances in the latter part of the eighteenth century which gave birth to the trade union and the labor movement. Even before the Constitution had been adopted, some New York workmen saw what was coming and organized in 1785 a society to forestall the wholesaler, the merchant capitalist, the middleman who invaded and destroyed the peace of the community market. About the same time other societies began to spring up rapidly. These organizations were made up of skilled workers only: like printers, shoemakers, tailors, and carpenters. All records of many of these early local labor societies have disappeared; but we know that the shoemakers of Philadelphia were organized in 1792; that the printers of New York had their Typographical Society as early as 1794 and were organized in Baltimore and Philadelphia during the opening years of the nineteenth century. The Boston printers were associated on a permanent basis in 1809, and in New Orleans a year later.

During the quarter of a century that followed the inauguration of Washington as first President of the United States in 1789, the skilled workmen of the American towns formed powerful local organizations to take part in the fixing of wages, hours, and the conditions of the industries generally. During the same period, trade unions drew slowly away from employers, finally excluding from membership those journeymen who became masters. In 1817 the New York printers expelled a member who had become an employer, saying: "This is a society of journeymen printers; and as the interests of the journeymen are separate and in some respects opposite to those of the employers we deem it improper that they should have any voice or influence in our deliberations."

These organizations of employees, united as a class to fight their own battles, were purely local associations of local workmen in specific trades. There was no consistent, combined action among the members of the several trade unions in any single town. The printers carried on their own affairs and the shoemakers theirs. They were not indifferent, of course, to the struggles of their fellow workmen of other crafts. There were correspondence and friendly co-operation among the various craft unions of a single city and among the unions of a single craft in several cities, but it was not until long afterward that strikes, politics, and battles against judicial decisions began to turn the minds of trade unionists to organization on a municipal, state, and national scale. The day of the great newspaper, the railway, and the telegraph had not yet arrived. Trade unionism was local and confined to separate crafts.

CHAPTER III

THE CENTURY-OLD TACTICS OF LABOR

Labor tactics as important as labor organization.
—An organization without policy and action is, of
course, powerless to accomplish results. Naturally,
therefore, the early local associations of craftsmen
had to decide just what methods they were to follow
in dealing with their employers. In the old days
when they worked side by side with the master, and
there were only a few in the shop, it was a simple
matter for them to talk over in a friendly way any
problems or differences that arose. As the cities
grew in size and the shops increased in number, as
the employees began firmly to close their unions
to masters, the question of how best to formulate
their demands, present them to their employers, and
enforce them became a live issue. One by one the
elements of the problem were worked out and a program of tactics and policies developed.

Collective bargaining.—Collective bargaining,
meaning negotiations carried on between employers
(or their representatives), on the one hand, and the
chosen representatives of the trade union, on the

19

other hand, appeared in the early days of the American labor movement. It is recorded that the first attempt at regular collective bargaining of this kind was made by the Philadelphia shoemakers in 1799 when a "deputation from the society waited upon the employers with an offer of compromise." In this case the employers said they would consider the offer and appointed a committee of their own to meet with the journeymen. In 1802 the printers and shoemakers of Philadelphia and the shoemakers of Pittsburgh sent a committee to visit various employers and confer with them over the wage scales.

In 1809, when the New York printers submitted their lists to the masters, this courteous reply came back from the employers' association: "In presenting [a set of resolutions] to the consideration of the Typographical society, they [the employers] think it proper to remark that, although no circumstances have come to their knowledge which would justify on the part of the journeymen a demand for more than the customary wages, yet, desirous of meeting them in the spirit of conciliation and harmony and to remove every obstacle that might have a tendency to interrupt a mutual good understanding, the master printers have made considerable advances on the prices hitherto given and to as great an extent as the present state of the printing business would admit. The scale which is now offered may therefore be considered as a maximum beyond which it would be highly injurious, if not ruinous, to the interests of the trade to venture." As a result of this courtesy on the part of the employing printers, committees representing both sides of the controversy met and finally agreed upon a compromise scale of wages. All over the country similar attempts were made so that we may say the nineteenth century opened with the principle of collective bargaining well understood in labor and employing circles and frequently applied in trade disputes.

Strikes.—The strike, meaning the action of workmen in quitting their employment in a body, is, of course, a natural corollary of organization and the formulation of demands as to wages and hours. Labor early recognized this fact. Ten years after the Declaration of American Independence in 1776, the printers of Philadelphia, after providing for a strike fund for the benefit of members, struck against their employers. In 1799 the skilled shoemakers of Baltimore and Pittsburgh struck for higher wages, against the competition of Lynn, Massachusetts, which had become a large center for the manufacture of coarse shoes—a center of cheap shoes and cheap labor. The practice thus early established was followed quite regularly when agreements over wages could not be reached by negotiations.

For the most part, it seems, these first trade disputes were conducted without any considerable disturbance. The journeymen simply remained away from work until the employers gave in, or they were compelled to yield, or a compromise was reached. Violence and intimidation did however occasionally appear, as in the case of the shoemakers' strike in Philadelphia in 1806 when "scabs were beaten and employers intimidated by demonstrations in front of the shop or by breaking shop windows."

The walking delegate.—As soon as a labor organization began to fix a "price list" or wage scale, it adopted the practice of sending the paper around to employers. One of the representatives of the union might "walk" around to see the masters. In 1800 the Franklin Typographical Society of New York drew up the first complete wage scale in the country and sent it to the individual employers of printers. Some labor societies selected "tramping committees" to visit the various shops to see whether the workmen in the unions were abiding by the wage scale and were "honest to the cause." This took a great deal of time and it was not thought fair to ask members to do such work without remuneration. As early as 1799, the Philadelphia shoemakers substituted one delegate for the committee and arranged to pay him for his labor. Thus the paid walking delegate appeared on the scene. It was a long time, however, before the tramping committee was entirely set aside in favor of the paid agent.

The closed shop.—The term "closed shop" is of

modern origin but the exclusive policy which it implies appeared in the labor movement as early as 1794 when the cordwainers of Philadelphia and elsewhere compelled each employer to retain none but union members in his shop. This was an old principle applied in the organization of guilds in the middle ages and by the lawyers and other professional classes. The Philadelphia, New York, and Pittsburgh cordwainers, as soon as they were well organized, required every member of the craft to join the society on entering the town. One manufacturer who refused to recognize only members of the cordwainers' society was forced to move out of Philadelphia after fighting the closed shop idea for a year and a half. Employers were sometimes compelled to pay fines to the union for employing non-union members. During a strike of the New York Cordwainers in 1810, the lawyer for the society explained what the trouble was all about: "If the majority of the workmen were content with their wages, the majority would be harmless; but if an individual will seek to better himself at the expense of his fellows, when they are suffering privation to obtain better terms, it is not hard that they leave him to his employers; and the most inoffensive manner in which they can show their displeasure is by shaking the dust off their feet and leaving the shop where he is engaged."

The boycott.—This modern term means "to combine (a) in refusing to work for, buy from, sell to, give assistance to, or to have any dealings with; and (b) in preventing others from working for, buying from, selling to, assisting, or having any kind of dealings with" another person or company. The term originated in Ireland in 1880, but the practice which it implies appeared very early in the American labor movement in the form of discrimination against non-union workmen. The boycott of the non-union man was first applied, not to the master who employed him or to the goods he made, but to the boarding house where he ate. Social intercourse with him was forbidden. Sometimes he was roughly handled and compelled to pay a fine to the union for refusing to join.

Control over apprenticeship.—No union can effectively control wages without reference to the supply of trained workmen ready to enter the craft. For this reason, the American local unions, at the very outset, took a stand on apprenticeship. They naturally objected strenuously to the unskilled worker whose low standard tended to cut wages and bring about sharp competition both in the quality of work and the compensation received for it. The New York Typographical Society, for instance, in 1809, complained that "a superabundance of learners, runaway apprentices, and half-way journeymen as well as adults who had served less than half time at their trade, had a depressing effect upon the wages of full-fledged workers." In a like manner, the New York cordwainers protested against the way the masters crowded "their shops with more apprentices than they could instruct." The printers also protested against "taking full grown men [foreigners] as apprentices for some twelve or fifteen months when they are to be turned into the situations of the men who are masters of their business, which men are to be turned out of their places by miserable botches because they will work for what they can get." Attempts, however, to regulate apprenticeship were not very effective on account of the rapid growth of the population, the influx of foreigners, and the continual shifting of the people from city to city. The old English rule of "six year apprenticeship" was merely a custom more often neglected than observed. Labor unions struggled to maintain it, but they had varying success.

The minimum wage.—Skilled workers were forced to rely upon the minimum wage or standard piece rate as a means of defense against the inferior workman or half-trained apprentice. From the first they insisted upon a minimum wage below which no worker could fall, while the more skilled might rise above it if he could. If employers had to pay that wage they naturally would not choose unskilled workmen. The minimum wage was bound up also with the price for which the given product could be sold in the market. Workers refused to permit a master to sell his goods at such a price that the minimum wage could not be paid. This in effect merely meant continuing as far as possible the practice of the old days when master and men by agreement decided upon a "fair wage" and a "fair price" for the goods which they sold to their neighbors in the community, but it was only by a strong union that it could be maintained after the invasion of the market by the merchant capitalist and the factory system.

Employers' Associations.—It is sometimes said that employers' associations were older than trade unions and were formed for the purpose of cutting down wages. The evidence in the case, however, seems to point to the contrary. There were, it is true, employers' organizations very early in the history of the labor movement. The Master Cordwainers were organized in 1789, but their aim was rather to raise prices than to reduce wages. As soon as the wages question became serious, as the result of the formation of strong trade unions, organizations of masters were established to resist the demands of the workmen. When workers were scarce they negotiated with them in a conciliatory way. As the unions grew in strength the masters often sought an opportunity to "break them up altogether, root and branch." They advertised out of town for new workmen; they agreed among themselves to resist high wage scales; and they united in appealing to the courts for aid against employees' "conspiracies in restraint of trade," as they called strikes and concerted wage demands.

Labor's battles in the courts.— The contest between masters and trade unions was carried into the courts in Philadelphia as early as 1806, in New York in 1809, and in Pittsburgh in 1814. In the latter two cases it appears that the masters had raised considerable sums of money to aid in the prosecution of strikers for criminal conspiracy. There is no doubt that employers all over the country were interested in the outcome of the legal battles; for the reporter of the Pittsburgh case said in the preface to his report:

Perhaps he would not . . . have undertaken to report it, but for the pressing solicitations of many respectable Mechanics and Manufacturers. . . . The verdict of the jury is most important to the manufacturing interests of the community; it puts an end to those associations which have been so prejudicial to the successful enterprize of the capitalists of the western country. But this case is not important to this country alone; it proves beyond possibility of doubt that notwithstanding the adjudications in New York and Philadelphia, there still exist in those cities combinations which extend their deleterious influence to every part of the union. The inhabitants of those cities, the manufacturers particularly, are bound by their interests, as well as the duties they owe [the] community, to watch those combinations with a jealous eye, and to prosecute to conviction and subject to the penalties of the law, conspiracies so subversive to the best interests of the country.

The legal issue involved in the conspiracy cases was whether, in the absence of a statute or act of the legislature on the point, the old common law doctrine of England applied in this country; if it did, any combination of workmen to raise wages was to be regarded as a conspiracy against the public. On this point American citizens were divided. The Federalists, or conservative followers of Alexander Hamilton, held that the English law did apply in America. The followers of Jefferson, who were certainly radical in their opinion for their day, took the opposite view. Of six legal cases arising between 1806 and 1815, four were decided against the workmen. A Baltimore case ended in a verdict for the journeymen, and a Pittsburgh case resulted in a compromise in which the workmen in fact lost the strike and paid the costs of the legal battle.

The conviction of the union men in Philadelphia and New York was followed by a hot political dispute between the conservative Federalists and the radical Jeffersonian Democrats. Indeed, during the contest in the courts the Jeffersonian papers attacked the legal doctrine of English common law that combinations of workmen were in restraint of trade and therefore illegal. In the elections shortly afterward the issue was carried to the polls and the Jefferson-

ians succeeded in electing judges more favorable to
the contention of labor, but the contest was not closed
for all time.   On the contrary, it continued to be a
live question discussed with much passion whenever
strikes and labor disputes brought it to the front.

A careful analysis of the opinions expressed on
both sides in the early stages of the struggle shows
how old and American are many ideas that seem
strange, perverse, and perhaps alien in character to
those who do not know our history.   On behalf of
the employers who sought the dissolution of combinations of workmen formed to raise wages, it was
said: "Those best acquainted with our situation believe that manufactures will bye and bye become
one of its chief means of support.   A vast quantity
of manufactured articles are already exported to the
West Indies and the southern states; we rival supplies from England in many things and great sums
are annually received in return.   It is then proper
to support this manufacture.   Will you permit men
to destroy it, who have no permanent stake in the
city; men who can pack up their all in a knapsack
or carry them in their pockets to New York or Baltimore?"   Such was the impassioned declaration
of the prosecutor in the Philadelphia case.

The Pittsburgh judge in his charge to the jurors
warned them that such combinations would drive
manufacturing out of the city, adding: "Is this a
slight consideration in a manufacturing town?   And

can they be guiltless who enter into combinations which have a manifest tendency to produce such a result?" The jurors were furthermore reminded that they were consumers and that higher wages meant higher prices. They were told that liberty and equality were on the side of the employers. The prosecutors were represented as men who "merely stood as the guardians of the community from imposition and rapacity," upholding freedom and liberty against oppression by organized workmen.

The spokesmen of labor on their part also used arguments that seem to have a modern ring. They laid claim to the highest kind of patriotism. They argued that recognition of labor's claims "will increase our commerce, encourage our manufactures, and promote peace and prosperity." They said to the consumer:

Temptations are held out to procure a conviction. . . . You are told that you will get your cossacks and slippers made cheaper by convicting the defendants [the workmen]. . . . Rest assured that they will not fox a boot or heel tap a shoe, one farthing cheaper for a conviction . . . If you banish from this place (as it is morally certain you will) a great number of the best workmen, by a verdict of guilty, can you reasonably expect that labor will be cheaper? Will it not rise in value in exact proportion to the scarcity of hands and the demand for boots and shoes like every other article in the market?

Labor's advocate in Philadelphia in arguing for liberty and democracy declared: "I would not barter away our dear bought rights and American liberty for all the warehouses of London and Liverpool and the manufactures of Birmingham and Manchester; no, not if were to be added to them the gold of Mexico, the silver of Peru, and the diamonds of Brazil." The striking shoemakers under prosecution in Philadelphia, in a Jeffersonian newspaper, made their appeal for political support in this language: "The master shoemakers . . . who in truth live upon the work of our hands, are generally men of large property to whom the suspension of business, though it is a loss, is not so great a loss as the total suspension of the means of subsistence is to us who obtain our income from week to week. . . . The name of freedom is but a shadow, if for doing what the laws of our country authorize we are to have taskmasters to measure out our pittance of subsistence—if we are to be torn from our firesides for endeavoring to obtain a fair and just support for our families, and if we are to be treated as felons and murderers only for asserting our right to take or refuse what we deem an adequate reward for our labor."

The outcome of the legal battle.—This contest was not without effect upon judicial opinion. In time the judges shifted their attention from the point as to whether a mere *combination* of workmen was

a conspiracy to the question of the *means* employed
by them to obtain their ends.   The right of journeymen to combine was quite widely recognized as lawful and proper; but strikes, boycotts, and attempts to
enforce their demands were still questioned and
made the subjects of legal action against trade
unions.   When strikers laid claims to their personal
liberties under the Constitution, they found much
popular support; but when they were represented as
oppressors of the poor whom they compelled to pay
increased prices for necessities, they found the popular verdict running against them.   So it may be
said that the outcome of the first phase of the labor
battle at law was the recognition of the right to
combine, leaving union men open to prosecution and
fines for employing methods that were deemed coercive by a judge and jury.   Labor had learned in this
process to take a hand in politics, to seek the support
of powerful partisan leaders, and to value the power
of public opinion in times of strikes, prosecutions,
and stress.

CHAPTER IV

LABOR'S FIRST POLITICAL EXPERI-
MENTS

Changing circumstances.—During the opening decades of the nineteenth century several things conspired to draw labor into political activities. In the first place, property qualifications on the right to vote, which had been imposed by the first state constitutions, were abandoned and the ballot put into the hands of practically every workingman.* In the second place, the prosecutions of labor unions in the courts of law had driven workingmen to a concerted action which rose above trade and craft lines. In the third place, the industrial revolution brought about by steam power and the factory system was making swift headway in creating great cities. It added rapidly to the number of industrial workers and created closer association among them. In the fourth place, the idea was being advanced that the hours of labor should be fixed universally at ten per day by legislation rather than by the painful method of the strike.

* C. A. Beard, *American Government and Politics*, Chap. **V**.

The appearance of political action.—The movement for separate political action on the part of
workmen started in Philadelphia in 1827. In that
year the carpenters were on strike for a ten-hour
day and all the organized workmen of the city came
together in sympathetic support of the movement.
Out of this interest in the carpenters' strike came
a city-wide union of unions called the "Mechanics'
Union of Trade Associations." Unorganized workers were urged to combine along craft lines and join
the central body. This new association adopted a
constitution in which its objects were set forth:

The real object of this association is to avert, if possible, the desolating evils which must inevitably arise
from a depreciation of the intrinsic value of human
labor; to raise the mechanical and productive classes to
that condition of true independence and equality
which their practical skill and ingenuity, their immense
utility to the nation and their growing intelligence are
beginning imperiously to demand; to promote, equally,
the happiness, prosperity and welfare of the whole community—to aid in conferring a due and full proportion
of that invaluable promoter of happiness, leisure, upon
all its useful members; and to assist, in conjunction with
such other institutions of this nature as shall hereafter
be formed throughout the union, in establishing a just
balance of power, both mental, moral, political and scientific, between all the various classes and individuals
which constitute society at large.

The transition from this strong union for common purposes to union for political action was easy and was soon made. In May, 1828, the Mechanics' Union proposed to the several trade societies that they join in nominating candidates to "represent the interest of the working classes" in the city council and the state legislature. The proposal was enthusiastically approved. Candidates were nominated and a large number of them, endorsed by either the Jacksonian Democratic party or the Federal party, were elected. Candidates of the other parties were forced to bid for the labor vote and a distinctly labor turn was given to the politics of Philadelphia for three years.

The example set by Philadelphia workmen was soon followed in New York, Boston, Albany, and other leading industrial centers. Candidates were nominated and several of them were elected to local offices. In New York a meeting of mechanics called to support the ten-hour day which had just been secured was transformed into a political meeting and became the germ of the local party organization. In New England an effort was made to combine all the workers, including factory operatives, into one big economic and political union, under the direction of the New England Association of Farmers, Mechanics, and Other Workingmen. This Association also planned a nation-wide economic and political movement.

In at least fifteen states local labor parties were formed; at least fifty labor papers were founded to voice the aims and demands of labor; political organizations along the old, familiar lines of county and ward committees and conventions were established; and radical agitators demanding revolutionary changes came to the front. The radical movement was, however, confined mainly to New York. In New England the labor leaders chose rather to prepare information and programs for legislators and to arouse popular support for labor's cause. Political clubs were formed for the study of constitutional, legal, and economic questions. Here and there candidates for the Congress of the United States were heckled by labor leaders; but for the most part their actions were confined to the local and state political field.

The philosophy of the political movement.—In the vast mass of newspapers, pamphlets, and political platforms issued by labor in this first political experiment there appears a vague class philosophy which betrayed a distrust of, and contempt for, the rich. Perhaps as good a statement of this early labor philosophy as any to be found is in the declaration of faith put out by the Workingmen's Republican Political Association of Penn Township in Philadelphia in 1830. It runs as follows:

There appears to exist two distinct classes, the rich and the poor; the oppressor and the oppressed; those

that live by their own labor, and they that live by the
labor of others; the aristocratic and the democratic; the
despotic and republican who are in direct opposition to
one another in their objects and pursuits; the one aspir-
ing to dignified station and offices of power, the other
seeking for an equality of state and advantage; the one
apparently desirous and determined to keep the people in
ignorance of their rights and privileges, that they may
live in ease and opulence at the expense of the labor and
industry of the others; the other showing that they are
acquainted with the nature of their rights, and are determined to maintain and possess them; the one seeking to
introduce and perpetuate amongst us invidious and artificial distinctions, unnatural and unjust inequalities,
while the other party declare that all men are created
free and equal, enjoying a perfect uniformity of rights
and privileges, and that unnatural and artificial distinctions, independent of merit, are pernicious in their
effects and deleterious in their consequences.

The practical program of the labor parties.—
When the workingmen descended from the realm of
high political speculation to state just what it was
they wanted, they found themselves in general agreement. Their demands included the ten-hour day,
the restriction of child labor, the abolition of the
old practice of hiring convicts out to contractors in
competition with honest and law-abiding workmen,
free and equal public education, the abolition of imprisonment for debt, the exemption of wages and
tools from seizure for debt, the establishment of the

right of mechanics to file liens on property to secure payment of their wages, and the abolition of sweat shops in homes and factories. To these demands a number of additional reforms were sometimes joined, including temperance, the abolition of lotteries, the abolition of capital punishment, the adoption of cheaper and simpler procedure in the courts of law, the abolition of monopolies, the prohibition of private banks empowered to issue paper currency, the abolition of compulsory militia service, the establishment of the right of the militiamen to elect their own officers, votes for women, and in many cases the adoption of free trade as the national policy in the place of protection.

The ten-hour day.—The most prominent of all the issues in this early political movement on the part of labor was the ten-hour day. It was supported by labor on economic and moral grounds. Particularly was it urged that long hours reduced workmen to the status of slaves, with neither time nor leisure to improve their minds or enjoy the benefits of civilization.

In opposition it was said that the movement for the shorter day was foreign in origin. The Master Carpenters of Boston, for example, declared that they could not believe "this project to have originated with any of the faithful and industrious sons of New England, but are compelled to consider it an evil of foreign growth and one which we hope and trust will not take root in the favoured soil of Massachusetts." In the second place the ten-hour day was combatted on strictly moral grounds. It was urged against it that it would open "a wide door for idleness and vice and finally commuting the present condition of the mechanical classes, made happy and prosperous by frugal, orderly, temperate, and ancient habits for that degraded state, by which in other countries, many of these classes are obliged to leave their homes, bringing with them their feelings and habits and a spirit of discontent and insubordination to which our native mechanics have hitherto been strangers."

In spite of this sharp opposition, the ten-hour day made headway. Outside of Boston it had become the standard day for municipal employees, and public sentiment was brought slowly around to the view that this proposal, which seemed radical in an age of twelve and fourteen hour days, was after all quite reasonable and proper. At length, in 1840, President Van Buren ordered the establishment of the ten-hour day on federal government work after a spirited threat of political action on the part of organized labor and political managers in touch with labor.

Free and equal education.—Although tradition has it that popular education was one of the original doctrines of the American people, in practice free and universal education did not get under way until near the middle of the nineteenth century and is by no means completely obtained at the present time. It is, in fact, largely to the agitation of organized labor in the twenties and thirties that we owe the beginning of the public school system. Labor leaders looked upon education as the real hope of working-men in their struggle to improve their lot, and in 1829 public education took its place at the head of the labor reforms demanded by the Workingmen's Party of Philadelphia. In March, 1834, the trades unions of the country, in a convention in New York City called to consider the "professional monopoly of education," urged the necessity of an "equal, uni-versal, Republican system of education." The next year the convention demanded the establishment of free libraries in towns and cities "for the use and benefit of mechanics and workingmen."

Labor never tired of pointing out the deficiencies in the educational system then existing. It called attention to the fact that public schools were frankly for the poor alone, and for the pauper poor at that. Such an ideal of education had a charitable flavor odious to American workingmen and inconsistent with democratic pretensions. It was in their opin-ion on a false basis and inadequate, being limited to "a simple acquaintance with words and ciphers." It left the great mass ignorant even of elementary mat-ters, there being 1,000,000 child illiterates in the country in 1833, New York alone having 80,000 of them. The Pennsylvania workers stated that in their whole commonwealth outside of Philadelphia, Pittsburgh, and Lancaster, no public education existed and that in those cities pauperism was its only foundation. They accordingly urged the establishment of infant schools, thus foreshadowing the modern kindergarten, manual training schools, and better instruction in order to produce as far as possible a "just disposition, virtuous habits, and rational self-governing character." The public school system advocated by them was to be supported by public taxation and to be extended to all classes alike so that no pupil need be labeled a pauper in order to obtain an elementary education.

Such a universal educational program, the early workers regarded as a panacea for all ills. For example, the Pennsylvania workers in 1830 declared:

All history corroborates the melancholy fact, that in proportion as the mass of the people becomes ignorant, misrule and anarchy ensue—their liberties are subverted, and tyrannic ambition has never failed to take advantage of their helpless condition. . . . Let the productive classes, then, unite for the preservation of their free institutions, and by procuring for all the children in the Commonwealth Republican Education, preserve our liberties from the dangers of foreign invasion or domestic infringement. . . . Our government is republican; our education should be equally so.

When the leaders in the labor movement came to discuss the fundamental ideas and purposes of education they found themselves very much divided. One faction headed by the educational reformer from England, Robert Dale Owen, demanded the establishment of public boarding schools where children would receive equal food and clothing, as well as instruction, where all distinctions of wealth would be swept away, and where children would all be taught mechanical and agricultural subjects as well as literary and scientific subjects. His idea was to use education to train the youth in community living and useful work. Against him was a large body of American labor leaders who advocated a more purely literary education, such as the well-to-do enjoyed in their schools and colleges, an education which would give the children of workingmen a chance to rise in the world and become leaders in law, medicine, the church. They resented the monopoly enjoyed by the rich and demanded equal opportunity for their children.

They were not, however, indifferent to the importance of education for citizenship. Even instruction in civics figured as a demand of labor as early as 1830 when the workingmen's party of Boston demanded "a diffusion of knowledge in the elements of those sciences which pertain to mechanical employments and to the politics of our common country." The Connecticut workers objected to a cate-

chism devised by the Puritan "ecclesiastical aristocracy," and insisted further on education in the
rights and duties of citizenship.   The Massachusetts
workers in 1834 were worried because "females in
an especial manner are educated to consider all useful employments or any avocation by which their
fair hands may contribute to their own support, to be
a positive degradation."   Thus the battle raged, con-
tributing powerfully to the ferment and public
interest which finally resulted in the foundation of
the free and equal public school system.

The radical agitators.—In this period when labor
was giving serious attention to political and social
questions, many radical agitators advocating revolutionary doctrines attached themselves to the labor
movement.   For example, Thomas Skidmore, a mechanic, was the leading radical propagandist in New
York.   He declared in favor of selling all private
property at public auction and dividing the proceeds
among the people.   As to agrarian matters, he advocated common ownership of the land and the
distribution of the general proceeds equally among
the members of the community.   Frances Wright,
from Great Britain, one of the first advocates of
woman suffrage in the New World, opened her campaign of public speaking on labor questions in this
period, arousing both intense opposition and warm
support.

Criticisms of the labor movement.—Even the

milder demands of the workingmen, to say nothing of the wild schemes of some who declared themselves the friends of labor, brought down upon the heads of all the labor leaders a terrible storm of abuse. They were called "Levelers," "Mob," "Rabble," "Dirty Shirt Party," "Tag, rag and bobtail," "Ring streaked and speckled rabble," "Anarchists," "Infidels," and "Communists" without much discrimination on the part of their enemies. In vain did the labor press disclaim the ideas that were ascribed to workingmen, attributing the abuse which they received to "aristocratic party editors," and the malice of their enemies.

Results of Labor's first political experiment.— The results of this first period of political agitation on the part of labor are difficult to trace in full. Many a positive outcome was seen, however, as measure after measure advocated by labor was eventually enacted into law by the state legislatures. Imprisonment for debt was abolished. The ten-hour day was accepted. The foundation of popular education was soon laid, and a magnificent public school system became in time the object of interest and pride in all parts of the country. Other reform measures steadily gained favor in the public eye. When the history of American law-making is written, it will be found that the invasion of labor into the field of political philosophy and action in the twenties and thirties was a powerful factor in shaping the course of legislation.

As to success at the polls, the labor movement had several victories to its credit. It elected many legislators and aldermen; it forced the old parties in some instances to nominate candidates acceptable to the labor party; it exerted a decided influence on the writing of the platforms of the other parties; it forced the politicians to give more attention to the matter of conciliating labor; it enabled many labor leaders to win a position of power in the councils of the old parties.

Nevertheless this political outburst proved to be temporary. It opened in 1827 and within five years had almost died away, at least as far as the nomination of candidates was concerned. In many campaigns labor candidates were defeated. At best, the results were local, temporary, and expensive in time, money and effort. The vote was a new weapon to most workingmen, and the immediate results were disappointing to their large hopes for some panacea. The slings and arrows which their opponents and the conservative press used against them were too strong for beginners in the art of political management. They were continually disconcerted by the politicians who used every conceivable weapon to weaken their influence. Their meetings were broken up by hoodlums arrayed by the politicians and in some cases by city officials. Seeds of dissension were sown in their ranks; they were deceived by flattery, frightened by threats, intimidated by abuse, lured away by promises of office and position. In the discussions of political and economic theories, their ranks were badly broken and their power in economic bargaining with their employers materially reduced. At all events after a few years' emphasis on politics, labor turned again to the field of industrial bargaining where simpler propositions relative to hours and wages involved few abstruse theories or doctrines.

CHAPTER V

RETURN TO DIRECT INDUSTRIAL ACTION

The effect of politics on labor unions.—Politics had swept away much of the machinery of the trade unions. A class movement had almost entirely superseded the trade and craft union movement. The Union of Mechanics of Philadelphia, for example, which had, in 1827, fifteen trade societies in its organization, had shrunk to four societies. Organization of workmen by wards and counties had taken the place of craft societies. The experience of Philadelphia was in a greater or lesser degree the experience in other cities. Hence labor leaders, when they turned away from politics to industrial action, had much of their work to do over.

New economic conditions to face.—During the years of political agitation, the growth of the manufacturing system had filled industry with young apprentices who were insufficiently trained and were undercutting in wages. Women also were invading industry, with the rise of the factory system. In 1837 there were about one hundred occupations in which women were engaged, working usually for

small wages and long hours. Evidently all the
"females" were not educated in idleness even in
New England. The economist, Mathew Carey, estimated that a woman without children could earn in
the needle trades no more than $58.50 a year and
a woman with children no more than $36.40 a year.
About the same time it was shown that there were
more than fifteen thousand women in the shoe industry of Massachusetts, hundreds of them earning
only from eight or ten cents a day to forty or fifty
cents. "In 1831, in the six New England states
and in New York, New Jersey, Pennsylvania,
Maryland, and Virginia, 58.1 per cent of all the
employees, including hand weavers in cotton mills,
were women, and seven per cent were children under
twelve years of age." The next year it was estimated that two-fifths of the whole number of persons
employed in factories in Massachusetts were children
under sixteen, and it was stated on good authority
that in many places apprentices were taken from the
poor houses to the factories. In addition to the invasion of women and children, there was the invasion
of the immigrants coming in ever increasing numbers to our shores. In 1832, Seth Luther, of Providence, R. I., who was one of the first to advocate
legislation for the benefit of labor, charged that
manufacturers sent "agents to Europe to induce foreigners to come here, to underwork American citizens, to support American industry and the Ameri-

can system." Prison labor competition, the wholesale buying and selling, and the division of work that
resulted from machine inventions to reduce skill itself all played their part in building up an economic
labor movement.

Rapid gains for trade unionism.—Although face
to face with hard problems, the organizers of labor
unions made steady progress during the thirties,
helped by high prices and fiat money.   By 1836
Philadelphia had fifty-three trade unions; Newark
and Boston sixteen each; Baltimore, twenty-three,
and New York, fifty-two.   It was then estimated
that union membership in the seaboard cities
amounted to 300,000.   In the meantime gains were
made in the organization of the women industrial
workers.   The men and women in the needle trades
of Baltimore formed a joint society in 1835.   In
the same year the Female Improvement Society of
the City and County of Philadelphia was formed,
including seamstresses, tailors, binders, milliners,
and other trades.   In each trade a committee was
formed which drew up a wage scale and won its acceptance by the manufacturers.   Women bookbinders in New York and shoe-binders at Lynn, Massachusetts, organized.

The establishment of central labor bodies.—As
organization advanced by leaps and bounds in the
individual trades, there developed a labor movement
of wider significance—namely, the combination of

the trade unions of a single city into central bodies
for financial and moral support during strikes.
These central bodies repudiated political action and
bent to the task of controlling the trades in such a
way as to improve their own economic conditions.
In their strikes for higher wages and shorter hours,
they sought to exercise some check on hasty and ill-
considered action on the part of any union.
Through common discussion of trade conditions in
different industries, the workers learned more about
the products of "unfair" shops other than their own
and thus they were able to introduce the boycott of
goods as well as the boycott of the "scab." The idea
of the union label now crept in so that workers might
recognize in the open market the products of union
shops and confine their purchases to such products
wherever possible.

Attempts at national unionism.—The labor movement of the thirties tried to reach out toward still
wider and more effective combinations through a
national organization of local unions. An attempt
in this direction was made in 1834 in New York
City when a convention was called from all parts
of the country "to advance the moral and intellectual
condition and pecuniary interests of the laboring
classes, promote the establishment of trades unions
in every section of the United States; and also to
publish and disseminate such information as may be
useful to mechanics and workingmen generally; and

tʊ unite and harmonize the efforts of all the productive classes of the country." Trade unionists from the leading cities came together in a similar convention for similar purposes for two succeeding years before they realized that their attempt to consolidate the workers of the nation was premature. They were finally convinced that better groundwork would have to be laid in local and city organizations before the national movement could become powerful and permanent.

Attempts to unify single trades on a national scale.—Astute leaders saw that before a national movement built upon the union of all workingmen could be founded, a number of separate craft organizations had to be developed; that is, each trade had to have its local branches in all manufacturing centers and these local branches had to be federated into a national union of the craft. Local unions of specific trades in each city had to precede the union of unions, or the city federation. In the same way a national union of all unions of the single craft had to precede the national union of all trade unionists. This first secure step toward nationalism was taken as the inevitable result of: (1) the attempt of employers to ship their work from organized to unorganized centers in times of strikes or high wage demands; and (2) the rapid growth of manufacturing in new centers. Craft union leaders responded quickly to these forces. During 1835-36, no less than five separate crafts or trades held national conventions of their own. These were the cordwainers, printers, comb makers, carpenters, and hand loom weavers. The growth of the railway facilitated correspondence and travel and made national conventions possible even for workingmen with small means.

Strikes and legal battles.—This burst of new unionism was accompanied, as may be imagined, by demands for higher wages and by strikes. Prices were rising with industrial prosperity and in every great industrial center workingmen were pressing their demands upon their employers. These demands were met by determined resistance on the part of manufacturers who were now better organized themselves and equipped with large funds to protect themselves against the unions.

In this wider swing, the unions also encountered again prosecutions for conspiracies in restraint of trade. Indeed a systematic effort was made to crush the unions during the years from 1829 to 1842 when there were at least eight important prosecutions for criminal conspiracy. In some trials, the workers won and in others they lost, but the inevitable agitation over the action of the courts followed. The newspapers were filled with discussions of the cases. The New York *Journal of Commerce* took the regulation employers' attitude: that trade unions injured trade and commerce, that they were not needed in this country, and that they merely represented foreign influences. The New York *Evening Post,* on the other hand, declared that "men must shut their eyes to events passing around them if they think it is a few foreigners or only foreigners that comprise our trades unions. It is a low calculation when we estimate that two-thirds of the workingmen in this city, numbering several thousand persons, belong to it." The official organ of the Trades Unions saw nothing but tyranny in a decision of the court against labor: "If an American judge will tell an American jury that these barriers which the poor have thrown up to protect themselves from the gnawing avarice of the rich are unlawful, then are the mechanics justified the same as our Fathers were justified in the days of revolution in 'Arming for Self-Defense.'" This was the signal for another battle in politics and at the polls.

CHAPTER VI

INDUSTRIAL PANIC, POLITICAL ACTION, AND UTOPIAS

The Great Panic of 1837.—The new unionism had not gone far on the road away from political action to industrial action before a severe industrial crisis broke in upon prosperity. In 1837 the whole financial system of the United States collapsed. England was in the throes of industrial distress at the same time and called upon American debtors, particularly the United States Bank, to pay their debts. Thus American credit was shaken to the foundation. Unable to dispose of their cotton cloth, the Northern mills shut down and closed their warehouses. To cap it all the wheat crop failed and the prices of foodstuffs soared. Wages were cut on all sides, plants were closed and workers turned out to starve. No less than 618 banks failed during the year. Whole towns like Haverhill, Massachusetts, utterly dependent upon a single industry, like the shoe industry, found their streets filled with unemployed begging for bread. Seamen, dock laborers, skilled mechanics, day laborers, all classes of workingmen and women were involved.

54

Effect of the panic on unions.—The effect of this industrial disaster on trade unions was instantaneous. Where union leaders were not condemned as conspirators for organizing workmen, they found themselves powerless to hold together unemployed men for the purpose of maintaining wages. They were forced, in spite of themselves, to accept reduced wages if employed, because everywhere outside of the plants there were hungry workers ready to take their places in case they struck. Out of work and out of funds, the unions fell to pieces. The remedy which the leaders offered seemed to starving workmen no remedy at all. Locals, city federations, and national craft unions all felt the depression. A few of them by desperate struggles survived the storm; but the labor press disappeared and there are left scant records of those troublous days to tell the story of the disaster that befell trade unionism.

The swing to politics again.—The almost complete destruction of the unions left the labor field once more to the reformers, politicians, and "intellectuals" who had other cures for the evils that beset labor. Although many labor men, in this period, turned to plans for forming co-operative societies of workmen and to futile experiments with the communist land colonies, it was politics and reform that occupied the center of the stage. Suffering from the ravages of a panic, the workers sought a remedy for that disease. They found that hundreds of railway,

gas, coal, banking, turnpike, and bridge companies
had been chartered in recent years, and so they con-
cluded that such monopolies were the chief cause of
their troubles.   They declared that the monopolies
drove employers, master mechanics, and small tradesmen out of business.   As many of these companies
made a practice of paying their employees in notes
that had to be cashed at banks at a considerable dis-
count, all the corporations and the banks came in for
a full share of denunciation on the part of labor.
Thus the courts, corporations, and banks fell under
the displeasure of the leaders in the industrial world.
The old political feeling kindled by the events of the
late twenties flamed up again.

The political movement of the panic period was
directly connected with the older political efforts
in New York.   Indeed, in 1835, the workmen of that
state had held a convention attended by ninety-three
delegates and had formed a political party "separate and distinct from all existing parties and factions in this state."   They rallied to their new party
(nicknamed "The Loco Focos") a considerable force
and put into the field a complete county, state, and
congressional ticket.   They were able to defeat the
local Democratic organization, Tammany Hall, in
a spirited campaign, making their drive mainly on
the monopolies and banks.   By this radical action
they divorced Tammany from the financial and aristocratic elements of New York City and forced it to

rely henceforward mainly upon the labor vote for its strength.

This political movement spread to Pennsylvania. A mass meeting was shortly held in Pittsburgh, and a trade union orator declared that the time had come for labor to turn to political action. "Trades unions and associations for the benefit of workingmen are good," he said, "so far as they go. They will at least ameliorate the effects of a bad state of society, but they are not adequate to the removal of the causes of oppression. This removal must be accomplished by the ballot boxes." The movement, however, exhausted itself in local politics and did not emerge into the field of national issues.

The outburst against the alien.—The unemployment, or "over-supply" of labor, which resulted from the panic of 1837, also revived the old feeling of native Americans against European immigrants. Notwithstanding the economic distress in America the stream of immigration increased almost steadily from year to year. In 1847 over 80,000 aliens arrived, and seven years later the number reached 427,000, to the great alarm of native workingmen. As many of the newcomers were Irish Catholics, labor leaders were worried lest an attack be made upon their new public school movement in the interests of religious schools. In 1847 a Native American party was formed to uphold Americanism against alien influence. It won some labor support and elected a few members of Congress from New York and Pennsylvania. A presidential candidate was also put forward in 1856 and a large vote was polled in the industrial states as well as the South and West. This movement made no deep impression upon labor politics and was without lasting significance in the labor world.

Labor and the public lands.—During the period of industrial depression and unemployment the attention of labor was forcibly drawn to the opportunities for independence offered by the public lands of the West which awaited settlement. In 1840, George Henry Evans, who had been prominent in the labor political movement in New York, published his *Origin and Progress of the Working Men's Party in New York,* and began to advocate the division of the land among the people on the ground that it was the gift of nature and belonged of right to all. Not long afterward he formed an "Agrarian League," with the avowed object of stopping the sale of public lands to companies and speculators and securing the apportionment of the lands in farms and small lots among actual settlers without charge. The idea was taken up all over the country and given various forms. At last it was made a national issue, winning the support of the Republican party in 1860 and bearing fruit in the enactment of the famous Free Homestead law of 1862. Prominent labor leaders served on the commit-

tees of the agrarian party and were influential in
directing the attention of the country to land reform. The support given by the labor leaders was
strengthened by the influence of the radical German
leaders who had been driven out of monarchical
Germany after the revolution of 1848. "If once the
soil is free, then every honest workingman will be
welcomed as a blessing to our republic," declared
a German communist, Kriege. Indeed, the land
reformers became so powerful in New York that
they threatened to dominate the labor unions, and
a resolution was introduced to exclude them from
membership in the unions. Writing in the New
York *Herald* on this point in 1850, James Gordon
Bennett prophesied the end of the labor movement
if the radical agrarians were not expelled:

A motion will be made to limit the membership to the
trades and thus to purge the body of men who have no
right to sit in it. If this motion be carried, it will make
a clean sweep of the politicians and socialists; and there
will be some chance of the sound wisdom of the honest
tradesmen having fair play to work out a practical redress of any real grievance under which they may labor.
But we fear the sinister influences are too strong in the
body, and the schemes too numerous, to allow that prop-
osition to prevail. If it should be defeated, then all hope
of accomplishing anything useful through this body is
lost, and it will fall into the hands of a few wire-pullers,
who will turn it to their own advantage, and sell the

trades to the highest bidder. Then will be acted over
again the farces already played in this city in which the
trades have been made the ladder of needy or ambitious
politicians, who kicked them away the moment they
gained the summit of their aspirations.

One year after this prophecy the agrarians were
expelled. The trade unions cast aside the reformers
and went over to Tammany Hall, giving political
strength to that organization.

Socialistic theories.—About the same time that
the agrarians attached themselves to the labor movement, another strong group of reformers appeared
on the horizon: the Utopian Socialists, followers of
the great French leader, Fourier, who was introduced to America by Albert Brisbane in his book
on the *Social Destiny of Man,* published in 1840.
Sponsors for this new appeal to labor denied the
theory of the class struggle against employers and
laughed at political action on the part of labor. For
the capitalist system of production and the isolated
farm, the Fourierists proposed to substitute the communist colony in which labor would be associated
with science and all things would be owned in common. Prominent intellectuals in the country, like
Horace Greeley, Charles A. Dana and John G. Whit-
tier, moved by the poverty and misery of the masses,
took up with this radical idea. Papers were founded,
sermons preached, lecturers sent through the country, and many communities organized with Brook

Farm as the model.   None of them lasted very long.

This "utopian" socialistic scheme, as it is called, did not prove attractive to labor although it was widely discussed in labor circles.   Trade unionists were not revolutionists.   They did not want to found Fourierist colonies.   They preferred to win concessions from employers in the form of shorter hours and better wages, and protective laws to cover their organizations.   Neither did the regular unionist take kindly to co-operative and profit-sharing schemes which the "intellectuals" offered them as panaceas. They had no capital to embark on production on their own account, and they were suspicious of profit sharing.   They were, however, constantly beset on every hand by the exponents of new and radical ideas and considerable energy continued to be diverted from the organization and management of unions into disputes over economic theories and land reform.

CHAPTER VII

TRADE UNIONISM AND THE CIVIL WAR

Industrial prosperity revives unionism.—In the late forties, industry was thoroughly revived: fires were lighted, wheels turned, and the machinery of production was set in motion. The effect of the discovery of gold in California was magical. Manufacturers drove ahead with new zeal, producing goods in vaster supplies than ever before. With opening trade, the demand for labor increased and the prices of commodities rose. This was just the opportunity for labor unions of the regular type. Promptly shedding most of the theories that had agitated them in the idler days of unemployment, they took up again the routine of organization with enthusiasm. "The skilled trades settled down to the cold business of getting more pay for themselves by means of permanent and exclusive organizations. Here begins that separation from common labor which eventually was to raise the pay of the skilled mechanic far above the level of immigrant competition and to distinguish American unionism from that of any other country. Instead of experiments in co-operation or leadership by humanitarians we now find rules for apprenticeship, the closed shop, minimum wage, time and method of payment, initiation fees, dues, funds for strike benefits, union employment offices and the exclusion of employers, politicians and friends of labor not actually working at the trade."

The old locals that had not perished in the panic of 1837 took on renewed life, new locals were established as industry spread, and new national unions of specific trades were founded. The Typographical Union created a national organization, holding a national convention in 1850 and perfecting its plans. Seven years later the Moulders' International Union and the National Union of Machinists and Blacksmiths were organized. The Stone Cutters entered the national field in 1853, and the Hat Finishers the next year.

In this period special efforts were made to bring into the union fold the alien workmen. In some instances men of several nationalities joined a single union as in the case of the Operative Bakers' Union with its American, German, English, Scotch and Irish members. In other cases it was found easier to form unions composed of members of a single race to expedite the transaction of business and avoid the tedium of translating proceedings back and forth into the different languages. At the same time attention was given to drawing the newly-arrived immigrant into the union ranks. The New York joiners and cabinetmakers in 1850 "moved and resolved that handbills of the Association should be posted in the Emigrant boarding houses in order to inform the newly arrived journeymen where they are to direct themselves in order to get work at adequate wages and to prevent their getting into the clutches of the working usurers." A motion was also adopted that like advertisements should be sent to the newspapers in Germany. All such efforts told upon the foreigner and brought him to the support of American unions.

New labor leadership.—With the growth of unionism, "pure and simple," came labor leaders of national standing and influence, men of great force as organizers, writers, and strike directors. Among them were W. H. Sylvis of the Iron Moulders and Jonathan Fincher of the Machinists. The management of societies embracing thousands of members, scattered from coast to coast, and carrying on constant negotiations with employers over technical points called for business ability and statesmanlike skill of the highest order.

Strikes.—The decade between 1850 and the Civil War was marked by strikes of greater frequency and magnitude, and this in spite of the fact that collective bargains were becoming more and more common in the leading trades. In the two years 1853-54, it is estimated there were about 400 separate strikes, twenty-five or thirty being on at one time in New

York City. Nearly every known craft from boiler-
makers to printers and coachmen was involved, and
scarcely a city escaped. In addition to the usual
disputes in New York, Boston, Baltimore, there
were strikes in Cincinnati, New Orleans, St. Louis,
and San Francisco.

The panic of 1857.—While labor was absorbed in
extending its organization and waging strikes to win
higher wages, as prices rose and the prosperity of
the country advanced, another industrial panic came
to paralyze business, in 1857. The conditions which
had always accompanied such disasters again appeared in the labor world: unemployment, wage
reductions, loss of membership, dissolution of local
unions, financial weakness and hopelessness among
those that survived.

The Civil War and the attitude of labor.—Before
industry had recovered from the disasters of 1857
the Civil War between the North and the Southern
slave states burst upon the nation. Labor was forced
to take a stand. Hitherto no uniform position had
been taken by labor leaders. Some of the workers,
especially the mill girls of Massachusetts, were aboli-
tionists; others were indifferent; still others sought
passionately to avoid a clash of arms. The moulders
of Kentucky, the moulders of Pennsylvania under
the leadership of Sylvis, and other organized workers agitated for a compromise which, in their opinion,
would avoid bloodshed; namely, the limitation of

slavery to the area it then occupied. They were opposed to the extension of slavery but anxious to avoid a fratricidal war. They tried to take the slavery question out of Congress.

Others were violently opposed to Lincoln and the new Republican party which was agitating the slavery question. Some labor leaders refused to grow excited about slavery. More than one of them said that the negro slave was better off than the starving wage workers. In this they did but echo the view of Southern slave owners who held that masters provided good food and clothing for their slaves and took care of them in sickness and old age; while under the factory system workers were paid just enough to live on and turned out to starve in hard times and in their old age. When the war actually broke out, however, and the call came for soldiers, organized labor ceased its active opposition, the leading labor opponent of the war, Sylvis, volunteering and serving as an officer in a company composed of his trade union brothers. All through the North labor rallied to the support of the government.

Effect of the war on industry.—The effect of the war on industry was felt at once. The demand for war supplies, iron, steel, and all kinds of manufactured goods, was enormous. Prices advanced, farmers became prosperous, discontinuing the attempts they had recently made at organization along trade union lines. Merchants secured huge contracts and by judicious management laid the foundations of great fortunes. Industries prospered under the high tariffs that were enacted, and accumulations of capital made possible the rapid expansion of industry.

Effect on labor.—Wage earners were the one class that remained at the same level of comfort or actually fell into a worse condition. They were now employed; but their wages did not keep pace with the rapidly rising prices of food and clothing. Merchants drove hard bargains with manufacturers in order that their profits on war contracts might be large. To get contracts at all manufacturers were thus forced to keep wages down. The opening of trunk railway lines enabled the wholesale contractor to operate over a national area and to bring unorganized labor into competition with organized labor. Stoves from Detroit were displayed beside stoves from Albany in the stores of St. Louis, and prices became the determining factor in survival. Even the government made no effort in the placing of its contracts to guarantee standard living and working conditions in the industries that executed the orders. Industries expanded so rapidly and the number of workmen increased so fast that the old unions were dazed for a time.

Labor rises to the necessity of the times.—Labor leaders confronted by such extraordinary war conditions saw, however, that they must increase their

efforts to extend the number of local unions and
enlarge the membership if they were to cope with
the situation. Slowly, too, wages rose on account
of the unprecedented demand for labor. With a view
to upholding wages and avoiding a crisis when the
labor market was glutted by returning soldiers, the
leaders redoubled their labors toward the end of the
war. The following table, showing the growth of
labor organization from December, 1863, to December, 1864, tells the story of their achievements:

State	Number of Unions	
	1863	1864
Connecticut	2	6
Delaware	..	1
Illinois	1	10
Indiana	3	17
Kentucky	2	8
Maine	1	7
Maryland	..	1
Massachusetts	17	42
Michigan	4	9
Missouri	4	9
New Hampshire	3	5
New Jersey	4	10
New York	16	74
Ohio	4	16
Pennsylvania	15	44
Rhode Island	1	7
Tennessee	..	2
Vermont	1	..
Virginia	1	1
Wisconsin	..	1
Total	79	270

The organization of local unions was followed by the establishment of more national unions. "During the period of intense business activity which lasted from 1863 to 1866 . . . ten national unions sprang up in two years: the Plasterers' National Union, the National Union of Journeymen Curriers, the Ship Carpenters' and Caulkers' International Union, the National Union of Cigar Makers, the Coach Makers' International Union, the Journeymen Painters' National Union, National Union of Heaters, Tailors' National Union, Carpenters' and Joiners' International Union, and Bricklayers' and Masons' International Union." At the close of the sixties there were in existence at least thirty-two national trade unions. Those that assumed the title "international" did so to include the locals organized in Canada.

The total membership of the trades unions at the time is a matter of dispute, but our most authoritative estimate places it at about 300,000 in 1872. The existence of 120 daily, weekly, and monthly journals testified to the vitality of the movement. Fincher's *Trades' Review,* edited by the secretary of the national machinists' and blacksmiths' union, was one of the ablest of these papers, and national in its appeal, advocating trade unionism, pure and simple, shorter hours, and co-operative production. The leading labor men of the period were W. H. Sylvis, of the moulders' union; R. F. Trevellick, of the ship carpenters and caulkers; Thomas Phillips, of the shoemakers'; and Ira Steward, the eight-hour agitator. Some of them were newcomers in the United States and all of them were unfamiliar with the history of labor in this country, naïvely regarding themselves as pioneers in many things which were really as old as the nation.

While extending the number of their locals, the trade unionists were busy pressing their demands for higher wages upon their employers. The following extract from Fincher's *Trades' Review,* of March, 1864, gives at a glance an idea of the kind of activity that engaged the attention of labor leaders during the war:

The State and Metal Roofers are organizing and it is thought they will demand $3 a day. The Segar makers are preparing to secure better wages. The Longshoremen have demanded $2.50 per day of nine hours, from the 7th inst. The Jewelers have decided to add 25 per cent to their wages. The Bricklayers demanded $2.50 per day, House Carpenters demand $2.50 per day, Painters $2.50 per day, Dry dock practical painters $2.50 per day, Plumbers $2.50 per day, Blue Stone Cutters and Flaggers, $2.50 per day. The Piano Forte makers demand an increase of 25 per cent on former wages. The Iron Moulders ask for 15 per cent advance. The Cabinetmakers and Tailors are also moving. The Carvers ask 15 per cent addition. The Shipwrights are preparing for a struggle. The Brush makers have been conceded 25 per cent advance in New York by all employers but three. Wheelwrights and Blacksmiths are in council. The Bookbinders are organized. The Coopers have obtained their increase recently sought and will make no immediate demand for change. The Coach Painters and Coach Trimmers will shortly remodel their list of prices. Several of the trades mentioned above have obtained the wages sought by amicable treaty; and let us hope that all may succeed without the resort of a strike.

The alien contract immigration law of 1864.— In order to meet the stringency in the labor market and to counteract the growing power of organized labor, Congress passed in 1864 an act authorizing persons to make contracts in foreign countries to import laborers into the United States, and bind them to work for a term until their passage was paid out of their wages. This law was a part of the price which farmers paid the manufacturers for the Homestead Act of 1862 which gave free land to actual settlers on government domain and thus drew labor out of the eastern mills to the western farms. Now the manufacturers were authorized to scour Europe for laborers to take the places of those who went into agriculture and to fill the new places created by the growth of industry. On the passage of the immigration act the American Emigrant Company was incorporated in Connecticut "to import laborers, especially skilled laborers, from Great Britain, Germany,

Belgium, France, Switzerland, Norway, and Sweden
for the manufacturers, railroad companies, and other
employers of labor in America." The wages of
laborers were to be attached until the expenses of
their importation were paid. This company was
composed of bankers, employers and politicians, and
was endorsed by leading governors, senators and edi·
tors—men like Chief Justice Chase of the United
States Supreme Court; Gideon Welles, Secretary of
the Navy; Henry Ward Beecher, the great Brooklyn
preacher, and Charles Sumner, senator from Massachusetts. Their advertisement stated: "A system so
complete has been put in operation here that miners,
mechanics (including workers in iron and steel of·
every class), weavers, and agricultural, railroad, and
other laborers, can now be procured without much
delay, in any numbers, at reasonable cost." The
result of this law was immediate. The stream of
immigration began to flow with extraordinary rapid-
ity. Labor now complained that it was face to face
with a growing "poor and dependent population"—
one whose "abject condition in their own country
made them tame, submissive, 'peaceable, orderly citizens,' who are willing to work for fourteen and sixteen hours a day for what capital sees fit to give
them."

**The National Labor Union—its program and con-
gresses (1866-72).**—All things conspired together in
war time to draw organized labor into closer union

on a national scale. By the end of the Civil War
every important city had its city trades assembly
representing all the organized crafts. It had co-
operative stores, free libraries and reading rooms,
legislative lobbies, and a labor press. It held
periodical meetings and helped those unions engaged
in contests for better conditions. There were, as we
have seen, about thirty powerful national unions of
specific trades and several of these trades had their
own journals.

The time seemed ripe for a grand consolidation of
all labor's forces, such as had been tried thirty years
before without permanent results. So in 1864
an attempt was made to federate the city trades
assemblies. A national convention was called for
this purpose, the idea being to form a national body
on the order of the "General Confederation of Labor
in France in which trades assemblies (*Bourses du
Travail*) and national trade unions are represented
on an equal footing." The main object of the promoters of this organization was to abolish strikes
and establish trade agreements with employers in
their place. In explanation of their objects, the
promoters declared "that the capitalists or employers will cease to refuse our just demands and will,
if we make any unreasonable demands, condescend
to come down on a level with us and by argument
and proof show us that our demands are unjust,
but this will have to be explained to the satisfaction

of the trades assembly of the city in which the demand was made."

W. H. Sylvis was the prime mover in this new attempt at nationalization, and he had the satisfaction of seeing a large and spirited "Industrial Assembly of North America" held at Louisville in 1864. Two years later, namely 1866, at Baltimore, the assembly organized the National Labor Union the same year that an international labor congress met at Geneva. "In 1867 the American organization met at Chicago, the European at Brussels. In 1869 the American organization met at Philadelphia and sent a delegate to the European meeting at Basle to discuss with it the question of European immigration and its competition with American labor. In 1870 the Franco-Prussian War interrupted the European congress and the next two years witnessed the dissolution of both organizations through internal dissensions—the American through the antagonism of the political actionists and trade unionists pure and simple; the European through the antagonism of socialists and anarchists." Socialists were the invaders in the case of the American movement; the anarchists were the invaders of the European movement, started by Karl Marx and other socialists. For six years, 1866 to 1872, there was a National Labor Union in America and each year a congress was held, dwindling to a handful at last.

The basis of the National Labor Union was the

city assemblies of trade unions. It did not represent strict craft unionism, therefore. Moreover, it
did not confine its efforts to the promotion of that
type of union effort. Sylvis, who was himself a
workingman and a good unionist, was deeply interested in freeing labor from the control of capitalists by means of co-operative shops in which the
workmen supplied their own capital and shared
the profits. In 1867 he declared: "At last, after
years of earnest effort and patient waiting and
constant preaching, co-operation is taking hold upon
the minds of our members and in many places very
little else is talked about." A year later he was still
urging the superior merits of co-operation as compared with unionism, insisting that unionism made
war upon the effects of industrial distress and did
not get at the cause, which was in fact the wages
system itself. Sylvis's own union, the iron moulders,
made a number of experiments in co-operative production, opening ten or more co-operative foundries
which failed. Similar attempts were made during
this period by other trades, bakers, shipwrights,
machinists, tailors, printers, needle women, etc. The
unsuccessful strikes carried on in 1867-68 were followed in many instances by the establishment of
independent co-operative shops in which the producer was to receive "the full product of his labor
and the wages struggle was to be eliminated."

One of the chief difficulties in the way of these

co-operative shops was that of securing capital or credit, and so the National Labor Union became interested in banking and currency. It therefore entered into relations with the farmers, the Grangers, and the other agrarians who were in favor of large issues of paper money, "greenbacks," such as had been issued during the Civil War.

Soon after the farmers appeared on the edge of the new national labor movement, women arrived on the scene. In 1868 women came as "delegates" to the New York convention. These delegates were not all workingwomen. Susan B. Anthony, the prominent suffragist, Mrs. Mary Kellog Putnam and Mrs. Mary McDowell came as representatives of workingwomen's protective associations. Elizabeth Cady Stanton was finally admitted from a woman suffrage society with the understanding that only her humanitarian interest in labor was endorsed. When it came to choosing an assistant secretary for the National Labor Union the convention selected a member of the laundry workers' union from Troy, Kate Mullaney. She was also made national organizer for women.

About the same time the negro question loomed on the horizon of the labor movement. Negroes had always been involved in labor questions in the North, and with emancipation their relations to craft unions and the labor movement became more pressing than

ever. Realizing the two-fold significance of the negro
as a laborer and a voter, the National Labor Union
decided that the negro's conciliatory attitude should
be met half way. In 1869 the negroes were trying
to form a national association of their own at Washington. The National Labor Union thereupon
resolved that "the interests of the workingmen in
America especially requires that the formation of
trades unions, eight-hour leagues, and other labor
organizations shall be encouraged among the colored
race." Accordingly it sent a friendly delegate to
the negro convention, Richard Trevellick, a prominent and trusted labor leader. The negroes wanted
co-operation with white labor, but gave special attention to petitioning Congress (1) for the exclusion of
coolie labor and (2) for a Homestead Act giving
land to negroes in the South. They also asserted
equal rights for themselves, with white workingmen,
approved co-operation, endorsed the eight-hour day,
but went no further. On account of their allegiance
to the Republican party they did not seek a close
alliance with the National Labor Union, which was
radical, independent, and sometimes socialistic, at
least in part of its leadership.

Among the many subjects to which the National
Labor Union gave special attention was the Chinese
question. Chinese exclusion was the first demand
of California unionists and was pressed on every

occasion until finally the Congress of the United States passed the Chinese exclusion act of 1882. Among the other demands of the National Labor Union was the eight-hour day and Congress passed a law establishing that as the standard day for federal employees in 1868. When certain federal officers reduced wages with the shortening of hours, the National Labor Union began to lobby to have the losses in wages made good; and, in 1872, a campaign year, Congress yielded to the pressure. The National Union also demanded the establishment of a government bureau of labor which was finally provided for in 1884, and expanded into the Department of Labor in 1913.

The decline of the National Labor Union.— Unluckily for the National Labor Union, most of the co-operative experiments on the part of workingmen failed, and the political gains made by agitation did not seem important or spectacular enough to hold the rank and file. The pure and simple unionists began to desert and by 1872 the Union ceased to function, having fallen almost entirely into the hands of political reformers. Another reason for its failure was its foundation upon city trades assemblies rather than upon the regular national craft unions. City assemblies were more interested in their local problems and in local politics than in national affairs. They found slight advantage in

the national enterprise.   More than ten years were
to elapse before Mr. Samuel Gompers and his labor
colleagues were to found the American Federation
of Labor upon an enduring basis.

CHAPTER VIII

A DECADE OF PANICS, POLITICS, AND LABOR CHAOS (1872-81)

A new attempt at unionism pure and simple.—
The failure of the National Labor Union induced
the leaders of four big national craft unions—the
iron moulders, machinists, coopers, and typographers
—to attempt nationalism on new lines. In 1873
they called a convention in which every protective
labor organization was invited to take part through
delegates. The new federation was not designed for
political purposes. The call declared: "The organization, when consummated, shall not, so far as in
our power to prevent, ever deteriorate into a political
party or become the tail to the kite of any political
party, or a refuge for played-out politicians, but
shall to all intents and purposes remain a purely
industrial association, having for its sole and only
object the securing to the producer his full share of
all he produces." Capital was not to be attacked
nor viewed as robbery; agrarian ideas were dis-
claimed; and all relation to communists disowned.
Theoretical panaceas were thrown aside and certain
practical propositions for legislative action advanced:

modification of conspiracy laws for the purpose of
giving labor a better legal status, exclusion of the
Chinese, restriction of monopolies, reduction of the
high cost of living, establishment of a federal bureau
of statistics, legalization of co-operative enterprises,
and regulation of apprenticeship. The convention
when assembled went on record in favor of straight
unionism, politics to be resorted to only when other
remedies failed. A vigorous campaign for the new
organization was launched at once, with a view to
making "The Industrial Brotherhood," as it was
called, a power in the industrial world.

The panic of 1873.—Just as the new unionist
organization was launched the panic of 1873 swept
over the country, opening a six-year period of industrial distress, strikes, labor disorders, and disasters
to unionism. With the paralysis of industry employers began to reduce wages and these reductions were
followed by prolonged and desperate strikes. Within
seven years, between 1873 and 1880, wages in the
textile districts were cut to almost one-half the
former standard. Similar action was taken in other
industries. Unemployment became so widespread
that strikes to maintain wages were perilous; where
they were attempted, lockouts usually followed.
Black lists and prosecutions intimidated labor leaders.
A successful national organization was out of the
question. The number of effective national craft
unions fell from about thirty to eight or nine and

even they were in dire financial straits. Where the national union did not vanish, its membership declined; the machinists lost two-thirds of their members; the cigarmakers, four-fifths; and the coopers nearly six-sevenths. It is estimated that the trade union membership in New York City fell from 44,000 to 5,000. In Cincinnati it dropped to about a thousand.

Violence.—In the anthracite coal regions of Pennsylvania, a spirit of violence appeared. After "the long strike which lasted from December, 1874, to June, 1875, and ended in the almost total destruction of the union, a 'crime wave' swept over the anthracite counties." A series of murders was attributed to an inner ring of managers who controlled the lodges of the Ancient Order of Hibernians in the anthracite district. These secret manipulators were known as the "Mollie Maguires." Their desperate deeds terrorized the region until the authorities of the state made a number of arrests and convictions. Ten ring leaders were executed and fourteen were sent to prison.

Two years later a number of railroad strikes were precipitated by the action of the Baltimore and Ohio Railroad Company in cutting wages. They spread to other lines and far into the Southwest, involving nearly all the great systems. In Pittsburgh the rioters got possession of the city and millions of dollars' worth of property was destroyed. Federal

troops were called out for the first time in industrial
disputes.   Labor leaders urged upon workmen the
desirability of preparing to resist by military organization the interference of the militia and regular
troops in labor disputes, and cities answered with
armories for the better management of troops.   Injunctions were issued by federal judges forbidding
workingmen to strike and their leaders to manage
strikes.   Thus labor for the first time collided with
the military and judicial branch of the government
on a large scale.   To many contemporary observers,
including John Hay, who had been Lincoln's secretary, it seemed that society was about to dissolve
in civil struggles.   It was then that the Knights of
Labor, of whom we shall hear more later, became
successful in secretly organizing workingmen to com-
bat the forces of capital in the industrial arena.

The entrance of politics.—The emergence of
leaders who sought relief in political action was again
due.   Labor was disorganized, unemployment and
poverty were widespread, labor believed itself outlawed, and unionism seemed to offer no safeguards
against such distress.   Workingmen's parties consequently began to appear in the industrial regions
and strong labor-political organizations, mainly
socialistic in character, spread through New York,
Pennsylvania, and Ohio.   Secret societies took the
place of open unions.   Underground propaganda
spread in all great industrial centers.   The farmers

likewise suffering from low prices for their produce appealed to labor to join in political action.

Indeed, before the panic of 1873 descended upon the country (namely in the campaign of 1872), there appeared a party of Labor Reformers who held their convention at Columbus, Ohio, and made an appeal, though with slight effect, to the labor vote. The farmers organized their National Greenback party in 1876 to favor paper money as the remedy. Two years later the farmers and representatives of labor met in Cleveland to form a National Party, which drew to its support some "radical business men and lawyers." The platform of the new party declared that "throughout our entire country the value of real estate is depreciated, industry paralyzed, trade depressed, business incomes and wages reduced, unparalleled distress inflicted upon the poorer and middle ranks of our people, the land filled with fraud, embezzlement, bankruptcy, crime, suffering, pauperism, and starvation. . . . This state of things has been brought about by legislation in the interest of and dictated by money-lenders, bankers, and bond holders." The distinctly labor remedies proposed were shorter hours of labor, national and state bureaus of labor and industrial statistics, the prohibition of contract prison labor, and the prohibition of the importation of servile labor. The enormous vote polled by the farmer and labor candidates for Congress in 1878 frightened the politicians of the two older parties into believing that a political revolution had come.

Many labor leaders gave up unionism and went over entirely to political action. Fehrenbach, the president of the machinists' and blacksmiths' national union, entered the Ohio legislature in 1876 and two years later was holding a federal office. H. J. Walls, secretary of the moulders' national union, became in 1877 the first commissioner of the Ohio bureau of labor and statistics. Foran, the president of the coopers' union, after experiments in politics, was admitted to the bar, and later entered Congress. The workingmen's party formed in California, under the leadership of Dennis Kearney, went into politics on the main issue of Chinese exclusion. The more radical trade unionists worked at local political organization, founding socialistic and communistic societies with a view to entering the national field later.

So the decade of the seventies closed with trade unionism, pure and simple, demoralized in organization and spirit, and politics occupying the center of the stage. If prosperity had not returned in 1879 and the farmers and workingmen had not fallen apart once more, a powerful labor-agrarian party might have played an important rôle in national politics. Prosperity was a signal for quietism on the part of the farmers and for efforts at organization to increase wages on the part of labor.

CHAPTER IX

RISE OF THE AMERICAN FEDERATION OF LABOR

Prosperity, the labor market and unionism.— With the return of prosperity, the money market eased, trade expanded from shore to shore, aided by immense grants of public lands to railways, industries responded quickly to the new demands for commodities, and immigrants began to pour into the country in ever larger streams. Labor now saw both an opportunity and a menace: an opportunity to participate, through renewed union organization, in the new prosperity, and a danger from a flood of unskilled and skilled immigrants.

New leaders arose among skilled workers, in the persons of Adolph Strasser and Samuel Gompers of the cigar makers' union, one of the few unions that had survived the panic, after a desperate battle with competition from tenement house cigar manufacturing. They bent their first efforts toward a reorganization of their own union on a British pattern. Under their plan (1) complete authority over the locals was given to the officers of the international union; (2) membership dues were increased to build up a large benefit fund; and (3) a benefit system was created to tide the union over periods of industrial depression. By a system of fund equalization, the well-to-do locals were obliged to help weaker locals in time of crisis. Here was statesmanship in organization of a new order—practical, businesslike, and substantial.

At the time this reorganization was effected there were in the country the following national trade unions:

Typographical (formed in 1850); Hat Finishers (1854); Iron Molders (1859); Locomotive Engineers (1863); Cigar Makers (1864); Bricklayers and Masons (1865); Silk and Fur Hat Finishers (1866); Railway Conductors (1868); Coopers (1870); German Typographia (1873); Locomotive Firemen (1873); Horseshoers (1874); Furniture Workers (1873); Iron and Steel Workers (1876); Granite Cutters (1877); Lake Seamen (1878); Cotton Mill Spinners (1878); New England Boot and Shoe Lasters (1879).

There was one single women's national union, the Daughters of St. Crispin, a union of women shoemakers organized in 1869 and in close co-operation with the men of the trade called the Knights of St. Crispin. After 1880 the number of national unions increased and membership enlarged rapidly. By 1884 there were at least 300,000 members in good standing.

The Federation of Organized Trades and Labor Unions (1881)—the precursor of the American Federation of Labor.—In 1881 a number of labor leaders, dissatisfied with the state of labor unions in the country, called a convention at Terre Haute, Indiana, which in turn called a second convention that met at Pittsburgh in the same year. At Pittsburgh there was formed a Federation of Organized Trades and Labor Unions of the United States and Canada. A large and varied group of delegates was in attendance. One hundred and seven of them represented eight national and international unions; forty-two were from local trades unions; three were from district assemblies of the Knights of Labor. The platform embodied political demands; such as, compulsory education laws, abolition of conspiracy laws as applied to trade unions, anti-contract immigration legislation, a protective tariff. The drift of opinion, in the new federation was, however, steadily toward pure unionism. At the third convention of the Federation held in New York in 1883 Samuel Gompers was elected chairman of the organization and of its legislative committee. The organization languished on account of lack of funds and lack of interest in legislation.

The American Federation of Labor (1886).—In 1886 five labor leaders, including A. Strasser of the cigar makers and W. H. Foster, secretary of the Federation of Organized Trades and Labor Unions, called a conference at Philadelphia, which in turn summoned a labor convention to meet at Columbus, Ohio, in December, 1886. To this convention came the delegates of the Federation of Organized Trades and Labor Unions and a large number of delegates from other labor organizations. On the second day an amalgamation was effected of the Federation and other labor bodies represented. The amalgamation took the name of "The American Federation of Labor." Practically the whole trade union movement of the country was there assembled for common action, "the delegates of twenty-five organizations representing a membership of 316,469 members in good standing," it was claimed. The great national unions, like the iron and steel workers, the boiler-makers, tailors, coal miners, and printers, were now brought into a permanent federation. The basic unit of the new Federation of Labor was the national or international trade union, local unions being allowed representation only while they were not organized nationally. A permanent revenue was provided by charter fees and by membership dues, a per capita tax being laid upon every unionist in good standing.

Samuel Gompers was elected president of the new Federation, a post which he held down to his death in 1924, with the exception of one year. From the first he insisted upon the national craft or trade union as the basis of the organization, and upon a sound financial policy, including benevolent and protective features and funds. In his second presidential address he said: "It is noticeable that a great reaction and steady disintegration is going on in most all organizations of labor which are not formed upon the basis that the experience of past failures teaches, namely, the benevolent as well as the protective features in the unions." The test of this principle came in the next panic—1892—when the unions for the first time in their history held their membership and strength during an industrial depression. Of this experience Mr. Gompers observed: "It is noteworthy that while in every industrial crisis the trade unions were literally mowed down and swept out of existence, the unions now in existence have manifested, not only the powers of resistance, but of stability and permanency." This result he ascribed to the system of high dues and benefits.

Firm adherence to fixed policy.—From the general lines of his fixed policy as to the basis of organization and financial methods, Mr. Gompers never departed. To them he stuck through "thick and thin." His tenacity was early tested in the great Homestead strike of 1892 when the Carnegie Steel Corporation demanded the dissolution of the Amalgamated Association of Iron and Steel Workers who had resisted a wage reduction. A pitched battle between the strikers on the one hand and Pinkerton detectives on the other hand, and a long strike involving much bitterness, ended in the defeat of the

unionists.   The country was then in the throes of
another industrial depression, and many baffled labor
leaders urged new tactics.   To the question, "Shall
we change our methods?" Mr. Gompers replied:

Many of our earnest friends in the labor movement . . . look upon some of the recent defeats and pre-
dict the annihilation of the economic effort of organized
labor—or the impotency of the economic organizations,
the trade unions—to cope with the great power of organized wealth. . . . It is not true that the economic effort has been a failure nor that the usefulness of the
economic organization is at an end.   It is true that in
several instances they have been defeated; but though
defeated, they are not conquered; the very fact that the
monopolistic and capitalist class having assumed the
aggressive, and after defeating the toilers in several contests, the wage-workers of our country have maintained
their organizations is the best proof of the power, influence and permanency of the trade unions.   They have
not been routed, they have merely retreated, and await a
better opportunity to obtain the improved conditions
which for the time they were deprived of. . . . What the
toilers need at this time is to answer the bitterness and
vindictiveness of the oppressor with Organization.

The development of American Federation policy.
—In the course of a few years after the foundation
of the Federation in 1886, a number of very definite
lines of policy and connection were formed.   These
may be briefly enumerated as follows:

1. *Avoidance of radical economic theories.* Although Mr. Gompers once remarked that "I believe with the most advanced thinkers as to ultimate ends, including the abolition of the wage-system," he did not allow his theories to interfere with the immediate ends of trade unionism. The American Federation accepted the prevailing mode of production: private ownership of land, private ownership of natural resources, private ownership of industries, and production for profit. The Federation sought to obtain for its membership within the existing system of production, high wages, short hours, and favorable conditions of work generally.

2. *The eight hour day.* The ideal of the eight hour day, which had been agitated long before the Civil War, was taken up by the Federation with great zeal as a unifying force. The cry was a slogan which went to the heart of every workingman. It needed no abstruse philosophy of society or economics by way of explanation. Mr. Gompers' constant argument was: "The answer to all opponents of the reduction of hours of labor could well be given in these words: 'that so long as there is one man who seeks employment and cannot obtain it, the hours of labor are too long.' Hundreds of thousands of our fellows through ever-increasing inventions and improvements in the modern methods of production, are rendered 'superfluous' and we must find employment for our wretched Brothers and Sisters by re-

ducing the hours of labor or we shall be overwhelmed and destroyed." The argument had passed from "leisure" to "making work."

3. *Co-operation with the National Civic Federation.* In keeping with its economic policy and its avoidance of entangling political alliances, the Federation naturally sought to win from the public and employers sympathy for its policy of upholding labor standards. It therefore welcomed the formation, in 1900, of the National Civic Federation, an association of prominent business men, financiers, and professional people. The idea of the new Association was to promote the acceptance of trade unionism as an essential part of the modern industrial system and to advocate trade agreements between employers and unions as the peaceful solution of industrial conflicts. Some labor leaders joined the Civic Federation with enthusiasm, counting these new friends as powerful aids in winning public approval for unionism. The meetings of the National Civic Federation, its literature, and its activities in behalf of the peaceful adjustment of wage disputes contributed very considerably to the success of the Federation of Labor.

4. *The trade agreement.* The national organization of labor and the national organization of employers developed together, the activities of one group instigating and stimulating the activities of the other. On both of them the extension of the market operated

to widen the field of their organization and work. Before the close of the Civil War several trades were well enough organized on both sides to permit representatives of capital and labor to enter into negotiations relative to working conditions throughout the country.

The method of negotiation by a committee representing labor and a committee representing employers was called "collective bargaining." The bargain that resulted from such a negotiation was called the "trade agreement." This trade agreement bound both sides alike—all workers in the trade and all employers. In several of the trades the organization was complete enough on both sides to be enforced without serious interference on the part of the unorganized elements.

The trade agreement presupposes a national union in the trade, a large membership, and funds with which to wage strikes. Such a condition compels a hearing on the part of employers. It presupposes also that the industry is highly centralized so that the employers can enforce the contract on their part against even the small employers who wish to carry on their business in their own way. It is not built upon arbitration but upon the theory of equality between partners to the contract. Trade after trade has accepted the trade-agreement method of adjusting disputes. In most cases, however, the agreement has been reached only after prolonged strikes and lockouts and heavy losses on both sides, demonstrating to each of the two contestants the strength of the other. The trade agreement has become a rather distinct feature of the American labor movement. It does not represent any revolutionary tendency in industry. It is based on the idea that labor shall accept the capitalist system of production and make terms of peace with it. It has been called "opportunistic bargaining" as distinct from revolutionary class warfare as waged by the radical unions of continental Europe.

The trade agreement is, of course, not always national in scope. It is frequently local and adapted to local conditions. An example of a local agreement is afforded by the building trades' "bargain" effected in New York City in December, 1919. The agreement provided for a forty-four hour week and a definite wage schedule. Among the terms of the understanding were the following provisions:

The unions as a whole, or as a single union, shall not order any strike against a member of the Building Trades Employers' Association, neither shall any number of union men leave the work of a member of the Building Trades Employers' Association, nor shall any member of the Building Trades Employers' Association lock out his employees; and, should any union, or the members of any union, violate this agreement, and the violation is not discontinued within one week from the time of notice of said violation is sent to the Building

Trades Council, it shall not be considered a violation if the Building Trades Employers' Association, or any member or members thereof, proceed to man the work with such men as can be secured, or, in case of such violation, if the Building Trades Employers' Association locks out the members of the defaulting union, or declares a general cessation of work.

It is further agreed that if workmen not members of the unions parties hereto are alleged to be employed on any job whereon any member or members of the Building Trades Employers' Association are doing work, it shall be brought immediately to the attention of the Board of Arbitration hereinafter provided for, and if the facts are found by said board to be as alleged, it shall not be deemed a violation of this agreement for any members of the unions above mentioned to refuse to work on the job in question, unless such workmen are justifiably employed in the case above provided for, that is, where a union, or a number of members of the union, have first violated this agreement.

To secure the fair and careful execution of trade agreements, permanent boards of arbitration are provided, representing both parties. To them are referred all disputes. The most significant feature of this process is the rôle of *impartial chairman;* many private citizens, drawn in from the outside to represent the "public," have served in this capacity with devotion and great success.

Growth of the American Federation of Labor.— When the Federation was organized in 1886 the actual membership was estimated at about 150,000. The growth up to the close of the century was slow, showing a total of 300,000 in 1899. At that point the membership began to swing upward rapidly, reaching 3,050,000 in 1919. If the depression after the war reduced the membership, the decade closing in 1925 showed a gain of nearly fifty per cent.

The American Federation of Labor as an organization.— The American Federation of Labor has its headquarters at Washington, D. C., in its own building, which cost nearly $200,000. Its officers consist of a president, eight vice-presidents, a secretary and a treasurer, all elected at the annual convention for the term of one year. These officers form the executive council. The Federation has five departments: building trades, metal trades, railway employees, mining, and union label. These departments were instituted in an effort to settle disputes that constantly arose between the craft unions over their respective jurisdictions. The field of the American Federation extends to Canada and the insular possessions of the United States.

The basis of the Federation, as indicated above, is the national or international union, the term "international" being used on account of the Canadian affiliation. City central bodies, state federations, local federations, and local unions not organized on a national basis are admitted to affiliation, but the fundamental basis is the national or international organization.

The national or international union holds its charter from the American Federation and in turn it charters local unions within the trade or craft. The charter held by the national union provides for virtual self-government, but the charter of the local union within the craft confers very little power of self-government upon the local executives. The national union is responsible for local strikes in the trade and for the success or the failure of the same. The executive officers of the national union may approve or disapprove of actions taken by local unions and may expel or disown a local union. Such breaks between national and local officers are matters of common occurrence.

There is considerable diversity of type among the national (or international) unions. The Typographical International, for example, is a strictly craft union. The United Mine Workers, on the other hand, includes every worker—all the coal workers, skilled and unskilled, who want to join the union. The latter type becomes more common in the fields of industry where there is a great concentration of capital and ownership.

The American Federation holds an annual convention composed of representatives apportioned on the following basis:

1. From national and international unions, for less than four thousand members, one delegate; eight thousand or more, three delegates; sixteen thousand or more, four delegates, and so on.

2. From central bodies, state federations, national departments, federal labor unions, and local unions having no national or international union, one delegate each; provided, however, that local and federal unions in any one city may unite in sending one delegate.

The current management of affairs is in the hands of the president and the executive council. It is the duty of the executive council: (1) to watch legislative measures directly affecting the interests of working people and to initiate whenever necessary such legislative action as the convention may direct; (2) to use every possible means to organize new local and international unions; and (3) to secure unity of action in trade disputes without interfering with the right of each trade to manage its own affairs.

The executive council, of eleven members, is a very powerful body. It cannot dominate of course the policy of any single trade union, but it wields a great influence on labor policy and action. It issues statements on public and labor questions from time to time. All important matters calling for convention action are first referred to it. It initiates most of the measures approved by the convention. It is composed of the master spirits of the Federation. It may levy funds within limits for the support of strikes and its hearty co-operation is important in the conduct of a big labor battle by any trade union, international or local.

Organized labor outside the Federation.—Besides the Federation there are four Brotherhoods of railway men; the locomotive engineers (1863), the railway conductors (1868), the locomotive firemen and engine men (1873) and the railroad trainmen (1883). The Brotherhoods came into existence as benevolent associations because it was difficult for railway men to secure acceptance by the regular insurance companies on account of the hazards of their calling. The insurance feature soon developed into an immense business, managed with skill and integrity. The engineers own their skyscraper office building in Cleveland which cost $1,250,000; they also own collieries in West Virginia, where they have themselves, as employers, been confronted with a labor issue. With a combined membership of about five hundred thousand, the Brotherhoods are powerful in their own position and a great factor in the total strength of organized labor, especially in times of co-operation with the Federation.

Having large funds to safeguard, the railway men have been extremely careful about using the strike as a weapon to enforce their demands. They have relied rather upon arbitration and the heavy pressure of strong organization to obtain their demands. Between 1907 and 1912 about sixty wage disputes were settled under the Erdman act passed by Congress to facilitate the peaceful adjustment of wage controversies. In addition to possessing huge funds, they are strengthened nationally by virtue of the essential character of their occupation. They do not depend upon local trades and local employers; their work is interstate in character; their national solidarity is a natural result.

There is also outside of the American Federation of Labor a strong insurgent union known as the Amalgamated Clothing Workers. This organization grew up in 1914 as a result of a rebellion within the ranks of the United Garment Workers, a union affiliated with the Federation. The leaders in this uprising were more radical in spirit and philosophy than their officers and the inevitable split occurred. In spite of its independent position, the Amalgamated grew by leaps and bounds and in 1920 it had about 150,000 members. Its leaders sought ways and means by which the union could aid in high production and obtain in return high wages and short hours. In 1919 they won a forty-four hour week for the members—a boon which few unions then enjoyed. While it increased its responsibility to the clothing industry by which it lived, the Amalgamated Union extended its economic operations into the fields of labor banking, credit, investment, purchasing and housing.

Organization of women.—The first national union to admit women on equal terms with men was the International Typographical Union in 1869 and the next year, 1870, Augusta Lewis was a delegate to its convention. Although the first women's strike had occurred in 1828, and was followed by several spirited struggles against wage cuts and for a ten-hour day, although women were active in the Knights of Labor, there was little stable organization among them by 1880. In 1892 the Federation of Labor put Mary Kenney in the field to organize women. A great impetus towards women's unions and women's participation in men's unions—such as we see to-day in the powerful International Ladies Garment Workers' Union—was then given by the Women's Trade Union League formed first in New York City and developed into a national organization in 1903 with headquarters at Chicago. It now has thirteen branches in the great industrial centers, and is seated in the conventions of the Federation as a fraternal organization. The League has helped weak unions and organized new ones, pushed protective legislation and created public opinion for its maintenance in times of crises, shared in the suffrage campaign, trained organizers, and stimulated the intellectual life of working women. The strongest women's unions owe much to its initiative.

CHAPTER X

THE AMERICAN FEDERATION OF LABOR AND POLITICS

The Henry George Campaign of 1886—Independent political action had been endorsed and tried many times and with varying results by organized labor when the American Federation of Labor was formed in 1886. The Federation represented, as we have seen, a return to economic action. Local unions, however, retained here and there their old political enthusiasm, although they were divided as to political tactics. Some of them bargained with the Democrats; others with the Republicans; and still others joined with the Socialists in an effort to form an independent party.

A striking example of labor in local politics was afforded by the spectacular campaign which Henry George waged in New York for the mayoralty in 1886. George was not a socialist, but relied upon the single tax as a panacea for poverty. He was not even a convinced trade unionist. Like George Henry Evans, the agrarian leader of the forties, he put his main emphasis upon private land ownership as the source of all evil.   He rallied to his support a number of middle class radicals and professional people and was nominated as the labor candidate for mayor.   George was joined in his campaign by Father McGlynn, an Irish priest who, after carrying with him most of his wage-earning parishioners and stirring the community to the depths, was excommunicated.

Organized labor was particularly active in this campaign because the New York unions had just been beaten in a legal battle in the courts.   For the use of the boycott they had been convicted in the courts and heavily fined.   They were now eager to turn to politics for redress.   Largely through their efforts, Henry George won second place in the race for mayor with a vote of 68,000 against 90,000 polled by Hewitt, the successful candidate.   As a result of the large vote, New York labor was encouraged by the experiment.   It had the satisfaction of seeing a long list of labor legislation pass the next session of the state legislature.   This list included the creation of "a board of mediation and arbitration, the regulation of tenement houses, provision for labeling and marketing convict-made goods, the perfection of the mechanics' lien, regulation of the employment of women and children, regulation of the hours of labor on the street, surface, and elevated railroads, the amendment of the notorious penal code by prohibiting employers, singly or combined, from coercing employees not to join a labor organization."

This labor uprising was, however, short-lived. George soon wearied of the name "labor" attached to the independent political party, and the demands of labor receded into the background. The intellectuals interested in a "panacea" grew lukewarm as labor pressed for more and more special legislation. Indeed, the call for the next convention contained so few references to labor demands that the socialists affiliated with it led an open war against the dominance of the movement by intellectuals. George himself preferred the name of "Free Soil" or "Free Land" party, and this widened the breach. The German unionists sided with the socialists, the local labor party was split open, and after a defeat in a second campaign, George withdrew from the field.

Attitude of the American Federation of Labor.— Mr. Gompers watched the political battle in New York with deep interest but refused to be overborne by it. He thus stated his position: "The labor movement, to succeed politically, must work for present and tangible results. While keeping in view a lofty ideal, we must advance towards it through practical steps, taken with intelligent regard for pressing needs. I believe with the most advanced thinkers as to ultimate ends, including the abolition of the wage-system. . . . As many of us understand it, Mr. George's theory of land taxation does

not promise present reform, nor an ultimate solution." He was confirmed in his strict union policy
by the wreck of the New York labor party organization. In refusing to allow the Federation to be
drawn officially into the work of forming an independent political party he followed a policy which
he believed to be justified by experience.

While the Federation abstained officially from
politics, many of its members continued to run for
office and local unions were more or less active in
politics. In 1894 the magazine of the Federation,
The Federationist, printed a list of 300 names of
trade unionists who were candidates for office. Of
this number only about half a dozen were actually
elected. Such experiments served also to confirm
Mr. Gompers as to the soundness of his position with
regard to independent political action.

**Attempts to drive the American Federation into
politics.**—It was not until the early nineties that a
national party projected along national lines and
appealing particularly to labor entered the political
lists—namely, the Socialist Labor Party, which presented a candidate for the presidency of the United
States in 1892. There had of course long been a
socialist movement but it had been local in activities
and organization. This Socialist Labor party sought
affiliation with the American Federation of Labor,
but was rejected on the ground that it was not a
trade union organization, as the constitution re-

quired. In 1894 the socialists attempted to secure
an endorsement of socialism at the hands of the
American Federation, and were again defeated. Mr.
Gompers led the fight against them, pointing out the
small labor vote and the recent defeat of the labor
and socialist candidates as proof that independent
political action was futile. With persistent regu-
larity the socialist members of the American Federation of Labor sought to secure from it a resolution
approving socialist doctrines and independent political action on the part of labor. Through thirty
years of presidency Mr. Gompers stood his ground,
winning at each successive convention the approval
of the rank and file in his organization.

**Legislative demands of the American Federation
involving political action.**—The refusal of the
American Federation of Labor to endorse socialism
and independent political action did not mean that
the Federation favored no measures which called for
action by state legislatures and the Congress of the
United States. From time to time the Federation
at its annual convention endorsed such proposals as
the initiative, referendum, and recall, the recall of
judges, popular election of United States senators,
workmen's compensation, restriction of immigration,
uniform laws protecting life and health, in mines and
factories, the establishment of state labor bureaus,
the establishment of a national Department of Labor,
restriction of convict labor, limitation of the use of

injunction in strikes, the exemption of trade unions
from the provisions of the Sherman anti-trust law
of 1890 which penalized combinations in restraint
of trade, woman suffrage by federal amendment
(1890), abolition of child labor, equal pay for equal
work (1894), the establishment of a national Department of Education, civic and political freedom for
public employees, exclusion of Oriental labor, employers' liability and safety laws, voluntary social
insurance, old age pensions (1909), government
ownership of the telegraphs, government ownership
or regulation of other utilities, opposition to anti-
strike legislation. It relied on persuasion and sought
to avoid political controversies.

The first battle over the injunction.—However,
labor again came into conflict with the courts. The
issue this time was the injunction. An injunction
is a bill or writ issued by a judge of a court ordering some person, corporation, or combinations of
persons to perform a certain act or series of acts
or to refrain from doing a certain thing or certain
things. The injunction is an ancient legal device
which came into prominence in the railway strike of
1877 and again in connection with the great Pullman
strike in Chicago in 1894. On the latter occasion
the local federal district judge issued a general or
blanket injunction to Eugene V. Debs and all other
persons involved in the labor dispute, ordering them
to refrain from interfering with the transmission of

mails or with interstate commerce in any form. The
leader, Mr. Debs, was arrested, fined and imprisoned for refusing to obey the judicial order. He was
punished for contempt of court, an action which did
not call for trial by jury but merely the hearing by
a judge.

Labor leaders were deeply moved by what they
called "a new form of judicial tyranny" by which
strikes might be broken through the imprisonment of
leaders without trial by jury. Accordingly the
power of the courts to issue injunctions was brought
into politics by organized labor. Although the
Republicans in their 1908 platform promised legislation restricting the use of the injunction, it was
the Democrats who inclined a more friendly ear to
labor's demand for drastic limitations on the issuance
of the writ by the courts. In 1896 the Democratic
platform denounced "government by injunction as
a new and highly dangerous form of oppression by
which federal judges, in contempt of the laws of
States and the rights of citizens, become at once
legislators, judges, and executioners." As a remedy
the Democrats promised to restrain by law the hands
of federal judges and to provide jury trial in contempt cases.

The campaign of 1896.—The more friendly attitude of the Democratic party in 1896 drew a large
support from labor ranks. At that time a radical
farmers' organization, the Populist party, was in

full swing with a number of ideas that were acceptable to organized labor. The nomination of Mr.
Bryan by the Democrats and his endorsement by the
majority of the Populists made a strong appeal to the
labor vote. In that campaign the Democrats vigorously denounced "capitalism and the money power,"
and arrayed the masses against the classes. They proposed income taxes on the rich, free silver or an
abundance of money in circulation, limitation of injunctions, and other measures which proved attractive to trade unionists in their struggle against powerful employers of labor, and especially against the
great trusts with which they had found themselves
unable to cope on equal terms. While Mr. Gompers
refused to permit the Federation to enter politics on
an independent basis, he privately worked for the
election of Mr. Bryan. At the close of the campaign
his conduct and policy were discussed at a secret session of the Federation officials and approved by the
members present. In 1908 Mr. Gompers came out
openly for Mr. Bryan, and boasted that eighty per
cent of the voting members of the American Federation had cast their ballots for the Democratic candidate. Two years later the Federation resolved to
"stand faithfully by our friends, oppose and defeat
our enemies, whether they be candidates for president, for Congress, or for other offices, whether executive, legislative or judicial."

This policy bore fruit in 1914 in the enactment of

the Clayton anti-trust law which severely limited the
use of injunctions in labor disputes and provided
trial by jury in case of contempt committed outside
of the court.   The measure was hailed by Mr. Gompers as a mighty triumph and "the Magna Charta
of labor."   His assurance on the point was somewhat shaken, however, in 1919, when Judge Ander-
son of the federal district court of Indiana issued
an injunction against the miners out on strike.   This
action was based on the Lever law passed during
the Great War for the purpose of preventing interference with industries, and curtailment of production.   The American Federation had been assured by
responsible officers in the federal government that the
law would not apply to labor unions.   What appeared
to be settled, therefore, was unsettled.

The collision with the Sherman anti-trust law.—
In 1890 Congress enacted the famous Sherman anti-
trust law, ostensibly directed against great trusts and
combinations in business, forbidding all combinations in restraint of interstate and foreign trade.
It was thought by labor leaders that Congress did
not intend to apply this law to labor unions, but
in the famous Danbury hatters' case started in the
federal court at Hartford, Connecticut, in 1903, they
learned that they were in error.   In this case the
Supreme Court of the United States on appeal found
for the first time "that boycotts could be reached
under the provisions of the Sherman anti-trust law,

and that labor unions, found guilty of combining to limit the market of goods transported from one state to another, were liable for the payment of threefold damages." [1] As a result of this action on the part of the court, the American Federation of Labor combined its war on the injunction with a battle against the Sherman anti-trust law. It succeeded, in 1914, in securing from Congress (among the terms of the Clayton act mentioned above) the exemption of unions from the operations of the Sherman law.

[1] See Laidler, *Boycotts and the Labor Struggle.*

CHAPTER XI

REVOLUTIONARY PHILOSOPHY AND TACTICS

1. MEANING OF THE TERM "REVOLUTIONARY"

The term "revolutionary" as used in this chapter is not confined to radical movements that seek to accomplish their purposes by bloodshed. The word revolution is often misunderstood. It does not always, or even mainly, imply terror and executions such as accompanied the French Revolution, nor the destruction of life and property by violence. There can be peaceful revolutions. The famous English political philosopher, Edmund Burke, once remarked that greater changes may sometimes be introduced into society insensibly through a period of years than can be wrought by sudden and violent action in a short time.

The word revolution means a fundamental or radical change in the basis of things. The winning of American independence was accomplished by a violent "revolution" which substituted the authority of the American people for that of the British King and Parliament. The gradual change from the agricultural and feudal society of the eighteenth century to the manufacturing society of the nineteenth century brought about by steam and machinery is called the "Industrial Revolution." Again when the old Federalist party was overthrown in 1800 by the triumph of Jeffersonian Democracy, the overturn was hailed as the "Great Revolution."

So there are revolutions that mean violence and bloodshed; there are revolutions that are brought about insensibly and gradually as coral reefs are built up by the action of tiny insects; and there are revolutions brought about by the political overthrow of a ruling class, such as a nobility or clergy. Changes deserve the name of revolution, however, only when they are radical, drastic, and far-reaching. The overthrow of a monarchy and the substitution of a republic is a revolution; the transformation of America from a purely agricultural country into a great manufacturing nation and a world power is a revolution; if the socialists should carry the election, find themselves in possession of the power of government, and introduce public ownership of natural resources and industries, that would be a revolution, even though no violence whatever might accompany the process.

Revolutionary labor movements as treated in this chapter are those which reject the present industrial system and propose drastic changes in the way in which food, clothing, and shelter are produced and the total product distributed among the producers. In the Middle Ages and on down to about the middle of the eighteenth century these things were produced by handworkers for use rather than for profit and the whole process of production was controlled by guilds and legislation. Then came the introduction of steam and machinery, the rise of the capitalist class, the industrial workers, world markets, industrial conflicts and many other manifestations of a new and revolutionary industrial order. Alexander Hamilton, in advocating the introduction of manufactures on a large scale into the United States, was in fact proposing a revolution in American affairs; while Thomas Jefferson, who wanted to keep workshops in Europe and America almost wholly agricultural, was in fact conservative. There have been revolutionary leaders in the labor world during the past hundred years who have wanted to go back to the old way of producing food, clothing and shelter, the way that prevailed in the age of handicrafts and the stagecoach. There have been other revolutionary leaders who have proposed to "move forward" as they call it into a new epoch in which the machinery of production shall belong not to private persons but to the workers collectively. Then there have been many irresponsible agitators filled with mere hatred of the existing order who have advocated destruction without offering any very definite program in return. A "revolutionist" may therefore be a very practical person; he may be a mere theorist; he may be prophesying something that is bound to come; or he may be a criminal. Whatever his type, he is always with us.

2. THE NOBLE ORDER OF KNIGHTS OF LABOR

The first revolutionary labor organization of national proportions and influence in the United States was the Noble Order of the Knights of Labor founded at Philadelphia in 1869 by Uriah Smith Stevens and other local garment workers. There had been revolutionary thinkers and agitators in the labor movement before this time—communists, cooperators, agrarians, and anarchists—but not until this date did a great organized movement appear.

Secret character of the organization.—The Knights were at first a local secret order. Their weird cabalistic signs chalked on the sidewalks and fences were as terrifying to the uninitiated as black hand characters of recent years. The ritual of the Knights declared that "open and public association having failed after a struggle of centuries to protect or advance the interests of labor, we have lawfully constituted this assembly and in using this power of organized effort and coöperation we but imitate the example of capital, for in all the multifarious branches of trade, capital has its combinations and whether intended or not it crushes the manly hopes

of labor and tramples poor humanity into the dust."
By maintaining secrecy the Knights hoped to keep
their organization "hedged about with the impene-
trable veil of ritual, sign, grip, and password, so
that no spy of the boss can find his way into the
lodge room to betray his fellows." Not until the
hostility of the Catholic Church, the press, and the
pulpit became bitter in the extreme did the Knights
give up the secret character of their organization in
1881.

The labor philosophy of the Knights of Labor.—
Like the Socialists, the Knights of Labor advocated
public ownership of all public utilities such as railways, waterworks, gas plants. They also believed
in adding, to public ownership of utilities, coöperative institutions for the production and distribution
of goods. Thus private organizations of working
people were to be coupled with government ownership in the new society which they hoped to create.

The form of organization of the Knights was simple. They believed that all laborers—skilled and
unskilled, men, women, whites, and blacks,—should
band together in one mighty organization without
distinctions of trade and craft. They believed that
this one great union should work for the coöperative commonwealth. "An injury to one is the concern of all" was their constant declaration of faith.

It was in their appeal to the lowest paid and unskilled workers that the Knights developed a menacing, revolutionary character. They naturally attracted radicals of all sorts, including non-wage-earning intellectuals who are always hovering on the edge of the labor world. Thus they drew to themselves advocates of all kinds of panaceas: greenbackism, coöperation, socialism, land reform, and other "isms." Not being bound down like the trade union to the routine of organization, dues collection, wage negotiations, and the like, the Knights gave free rein to their revolutionary speculations. They denied all identity of interest between the employer and employee, and proposed no collective bargaining as a means to industrial peace. "To point out a way to utterly destroy the [wage] system would be a pleasure to me," exclaimed Grand Master Workman Powderly, long a leader of the Knights.

Nevertheless, the bona fide working-class element in the Knights, forced by necessity to earn a livelihood in the prevailing system of production, constantly insisted on the importance of "getting down to earth," carrying on strikes for better wages, and making wage bargains with employers. This "practical" element got the upper hand in the decade of the eighties; but the theoreticians and utopians were always numerous and strong. Between the two the Noble Order was torn into shreds. The officers, caught between the two great factions, tried to ap-

pease both by political and humanitarian activities
on the one hand and economic warfare along wage
and trade union lines on the other hand.

The Knights in the national field.—The growth of
the Knights was slow at first. By 1873 they had
only six assemblies, all in Philadelphia. Then the
idea was taken up by workers in other cities and
steadily spread throughout the industrial regions.
In 1875 the Knights called a national convention at
Tyrone, Pennsylvania, extending an invitation to
other labor organizations to join with them. The
Social Democratic Party of North America, which
had just got under way, accepted the invitation.
Thus the socialists with their determined hostility
to the capitalist system of production actively participated for the first time as a group in the American labor movement.

Launched on a national scale, the Knights grew
by leaps and bounds in membership and strength.
They began an aggressive campaign for a higher
standard of living, waging strikes all along the line.
One of their most severe and successful contests was
with the Gould railway system in 1885. In this
battle they introduced *sabotage,* though that name
had not yet been chosen for this species of industrial
warfare; they disabled railway locomotives by re-
moving vital parts. Having crippled the railway
system they were able to win recognition and con-

cessions from the most powerful capitalist of the day, Jay Gould, and this stroke gave them a world-wide reputation for daring and industrial power. Their triumph was received with alarm and amazement by the press and the public at large. The rank and file declared that the Gould strike represented merely a phase in the "deadly conflict" between capital and labor. So radical did they become that they swept aside the officials who sought to restrain their revolutionary ardor. Even the loss of a number of strikes about the same time did not convince them that there were limits to the possibilities of their order.

The conflict of the Knights with the American Federation of Labor.—Just at this period the American Federation of Labor entered the field, based upon ideas directly opposite to those held by the Knights, namely, the craft or trade union (excluding the unorganized and unskilled), wage bargaining, and abstention from political action and revolutionary theories. In 1886 the two organizations had a membership of nearly a million, of whom about 700,000 were Knights. The latter, much stronger from the standpoint of numbers, were primarily interested in the unskilled. If necessary, they were prepared to level the skilled down in their efforts to raise the casual laborer. The Knights, however, tried to win and hold the sympathy and support of the skilled craft unionists, because they knew that without the aid of the latter they could not go far. Historically, as we have seen, the skilled craftsman resented the invasion of industry by the unskilled adult and the untrained apprentice, so that it was no mean task that the Knights set before themselves.

In this contest the skilled workers steadily refused amalgamation with the Knights, the weaker element in industry, insisting that such a union would retard their own development.   The fate of the skilled craftsmen was too uncertain at this period for them to risk an expansion over the whole industrial field.   They held from the beginning that the tendency of the skilled trades was "to sink to the level of pauper labor."   Self-preservation had been their instinct and in 1886 they firmly took this position: "To protect the skilled labor of America from being reduced to beggary and to sustain the standard of American workmanship and skill, the trades unions of America have been established."   To dilute the craft union with a floating mass of unskilled labor seemed to them to be the beginning of ruin for all labor.

In vain did the Knights seek to win craft support. In 1886 they appealed to the iron and steel workers in the following language: "In the use of the wonderful inventions . . . your organization plays a most important part. Naturally it embraces within its ranks a very large proportion of laborers of a high grade of skill and intelligence. With this skill of hand, guided by intelligent thought, comes the right to demand that excess of compensation paid to skilled above the unskilled labor. But the unskilled labor must receive attention, or in the hour of difficulty the employer will not hesitate to use it to depress the compensation you receive. That skilled or unskilled labor may no longer be found unorganized, we ask of you to annex your grand and powerful corps to the main army that we may fight the battle under one flag."

The appeal was without effect. Efforts were then made at coöperation in the form of "the interchange of working cards, the adoption of some plan by which all labor organizations could be protected from unfair men, men expelled, suspended, under fine if guilty of taking places of union men or Knights of Labor while on strike or while locked out from work, the adoption of a uniform standard of hours and wages . . . a system of joint conferences and of common action against employers provided that in the settlement of any difficulties between employers and employees the organizations represented in the establishment shall be parties to the settlement." Such coöperation was difficult, for the non-union goods condemned by the regular unionists were often made by Knights of Labor. Thus the two organizations really "scabbed" on each other, and friction was constant. In October, 1886, the Knights declared open war on the American Federation of Labor which in turn quickly retaliated.

Decline of the Knights of Labor.—At war with powerful craft unions, left to themselves in the industrial field, the Knights rapidly disintegrated. Their aggressive strikes generally failed. Arbitration was refused by employers who used the "blacklist," the "ironclad" (an oath never to belong to any labor organization), and Pinkerton detectives to defeat them. The Pinkerton agency was really the most effective repressive force. The agency advertised among employers that "corporations and individuals desirous of ascertaining the feeling of their employees and whether they are likely to engage in strikes or are joining any secret labor organization with a view of compelling terms from corporations or employers, can obtain, on application to the superintendent of either of the offices, a detective suitable to associate with their employees and obtain this information." Thus the spy system which had brought into being the secret Order of the Knights of Labor continued and even outlived the society founded to resist it.

In spite of their difficulties, however, the Knights had done much successful organization work in their time. Many weak unions such as the barbers, horse railway men, miners, trunk makers, and harness-makers had been reorganized by the Knights and put on their feet. The United Brewery Workers, established in 1884, was among the strongest units in the Order. In 1893 the United Hebrew Trades of New York City joined. So effective had been the work of the Knights that many of their unions, including some industrial unions and some unions of semi-skilled workers, were taken into the American Federation of Labor. Moreover, the Federation was often forced to adapt industrial unionism to what it has called "federal unions"; that is, unions of city workers representing miscellaneous trades no one of which has its own national craft union.

The Knights also exercised influence upon legislation. They were successful lobbyists and were mainly responsible for the first restrictive immigration law—the Anti-Contract labor law of February 2, 1885—and for a considerable body of state labor legislation. Though the Knights were not in favor of strict apprenticeship laws such as were advocated by the skilled trade unionists, they were against the use of strike breakers introduced into the country by contract and in favor of other measures beneficial to the whole group of American laborers.

Coöperation which had been among the first ideas of the Knights was never neglected. Many Knights, especially among the men whose skill was menaced by the introduction of machinery, bent all their efforts toward productive coöperation.[1] This wing of the Knights had not been "class conscious," for it was composed of men who aspired to be small employers or were actually employers. They had gone into the organization in the hope that the whole weight of the Knights would be turned to organizing coöperative societies. Whenever strikes failed or industrial depression set in, there would come a wave of enthusiasm for forming small productive shops owned and operated by groups of workmen themselves. Sometimes, as the Illinois Commissioner of Labor said, "wage earners are forced into coöperation by reason of discrimination against

---

[1] The following list of coöperative societies founded in the period of the Knights of Labor is representative if not complete:

Mining	22	Carpentering	2
Coopers	15	Laundries	2
Shoes	14	Carpets	1
Clothing	8	Bakers	1
Foundries	8	Leather	1
Soap	6	Leather goods	1
Furniture workers	5	Plumbing	1
Cigar	5	Harness	1
Glass	5	Watch cases	1
Knitting	3	Pipes	1
Nail mills	3	Brass works	1
Tobacco	3	Pottery	1
Planing mills	3	Wagon	1
Tailoring	2	Refining	1
Hats	2	Caskets	1
Printing	2	Brooms	1
Agricultural implements	2	Pottery	1
Painters	2	Ice	1
Matches	2	Packing	1
Baking powder	2		
		Total	135

them by employers. Especially is this true of productive enterprises, many of which are the direct result of unsuccessful strikes and blacklisting which has followed them."

Most of these coöperative enterprises failed for one reason or another, the successful experiments apparently being joint stock companies rather than the coöperative brotherhoods organized along idealistic lines. In spite of heroic efforts on the part of Knights to educate their members in the principles of coöperation, enthusiasm waned among organized workmen. At all events it no longer appeared as a panacea. Thus defeated in the attempts to conquer the capitalist system by coöperation, at war with powerful craft unions organized under the American Federation of Labor, the Knights disappeared in the nineties. So the first "grand national union of industrial workers," all inclusive and revolutionary, passed into the limbo of dead experiments. The American Federation of Labor and skilled workers held the field.

3. THE SOCIALIST MOVEMENT

Socialism is a vague term which has a different meaning from age to age and from group to group. Its essential implication, however, is clear: it proposes to substitute some form of collective ownership of the means of production and distribution for

the present system of private ownership. Some
socialists believe that the *instrument* through which
collective ownership is to be effected and carried on
is the state or the government as it now exists.
These are state socialists. Others believe that each
great group of workers should own and manage the
resources and machinery with which they work;
that is, the miners should own the mines, the railway
men the railways, and so on. Such is, in short, the
faith of the "guild socialists." Still others hold the
present political state or government will come to
an end and a new collective organ be substituted for
it, like a "soviet," or council of delegates from
groups of workers and farmers. It will be seen
that the essence of all these plans is the abolition
of private property in the fundamental means of
production and the substitution of collective ownership, management, and distribution. Whether the
instrument is the government, the guild or the soviet,
it is a collective body representing the workers collectively, or a federation of groups or crafts.

If socialists are divided as to the meaning of the
term, so also are they divided as to the methods by
which the socialist commonwealth is to be brought
about. Some hold that it is to be accomplished by
education and agitation; that a sufficient majority of
the people are to be converted to the socialist view;
and that legislative and administrative action is to
bring the instruments of production and distribution

under collective ownership and operation. Those who advocate such tactics point to the way in which municipalities take over and operate their electric light plants, the state constructs grain elevators, or the federal government enters into the parcels post business. Carry this line of governmental activity, such socialists say, to its logical conclusion, and you have a socialist state.

Other adherents to socialist doctrines maintain that the transition to the collective or coöperative society will come only through the action of powerful industrial or trades unions which will paralyze the existing system by strikes or violence and then take possession of the instruments of production and distribution. Nearly all socialists, even state or political socialists, believe that the trade or industrial union will be an essential part of the new order of society whatever it may be. In short, socialism is to be adopted in the interest primarily of the working classes and the economic system established is to be managed by them.

The Utopian Socialists.—The socialistic theory of society is almost as old as civilization. It is set forth in *The Republic,* written by the great Greek philosopher, Plato, in the fourth century before Christ; it is sketched in the *Utopia* of Sir Thomas More, written in 1516; and in many other famous books that have appeared since that time.

The first of the leading socialists in the modern

industrial age was Robert Owen, a wealthy English manufacturer who, oppressed by the misery and poverty which he saw about him, sought for a remedy. This remedy he found in the formation of coöperative communities having land and tools sufficient in the main for their support and producing by common labor all the food and clothing necessary for the members. He proposed to bring about his system gradually and by converting rich and educated men to his doctrines. Owen came to this country in 1825 and founded one of his colonies at New Harmony, Indiana, but it soon failed through internal dissensions. Then Owen's son, Robert Dale Owen, began a propaganda in America for a state socialist scheme of education, and attracted to himself a number of leaders in the labor world who were working for a system of universal education. Owen and Frances Wright, one of the humanitarians of her day, carried on a vigorous agitation for education and for a complete program of legislation in the interests of labor. "Fanny Wright" societies sprang up all through the country and largely through her influence labor was drawn into its first political experiments in the late twenties.

Similar in character to the Owen coöperative scheme was the plan of Fourier (a French socialist), advocated in America by Albert Brisbane, among others, in the thirties and forties. As a result of this ferment, socialistic colonies sprang up in different parts of the country, and many leading men, especially in New England, called themselves socialists. Through three years beginning in 1841, Horace Greeley ran in the New York *Tribune* a series of articles advocating Fourier's ideas. Greeley was himself associated with the "socialists" of that day and published in his *Recollections of a Busy Life* two interesting chapters setting forth his views.

The Marxian Socialists.—Socialism entered upon a new phase in America in the late forties and fifties when radical German refugees, fleeing from the persecution of the Prussian government that followed the disastrous revolution of 1848, began to come to the United States in large numbers. About the same time, two Germans, Karl Marx and Friedrich Engels, issued the famous "Communist Manifesto," setting forth a new and radical view of socialism. They declared that all history was the history of class struggles and that the modern struggle between the capitalists and laborers would end in the triumph of the latter and the establishment of a socialist society. Marx did not propose to rely, like Robert Owen, on persuading people to work for and establish, out of the goodness of their hearts, an ideal commonwealth. He prophesied that it would come out of the class conflict and urged workingmen to help on the process. From the point of view of

Marx there could be no final partnership between capital and labor.

In 1864, the International Workingmen's Association was founded by Marx and the British trade unions to assist the unions of European countries in their efforts to prevent "scabbing" by immigrant labor. In this subject, American labor men were deeply concerned. W. H. Sylvis, an American labor leader, who had tried to nationalize the unionist movement here, attempted also to bring American organized labor into relations with the international movement. When, in 1867, the International Workingmen's Association deserted Marxism for a time and went over to political action along lines advocated by another German leader, Ferdinand Lassalle, the American labor movement took a similar turn. The National Labor Union, Sylvis' enterprise (see page 72), was political in its purposes though it was not socialist in its doctrines.

Unable to create a national socialist party, American workingmen of radical or socialistic tendencies kept closely in touch with European movements and theories. They formed several socialist local branches of the International Workingmen's Association before 1872. These branches started with German groups and then included French and Bohemian groups. In 1871 eight such locals with a membership of 293 members were reported. An American section founded in 1870 claimed to be "the direct successor if not the actual continuator of the industrial congress and labor and land reform movement of twenty and twenty-five years ago." This American local embraced quite a number of "intellectuals." At the European conference of 1872 the view was generally held that "the native Americans were all speculators and that the immigrants alone constituted the wage-earning class in America." To save the International from the control of anarchists in 1872, the conservative socialists transferred its headquarters to New York, and "the father of American socialism," F. A. Sorge, carried on in this country the fight against attempts of the anarchists to get possession of the socialist movement. In 1873 the German section established a weekly paper, the *Arbeiter-Zeitung*.

The first attempt to unify and Americanize the socialist locals was made at a convention held in New York in 1874. At this conference an effort was made to combine trade unionism with political action. On this point the convention declared: "The trade union is the cradle of the labor movement, for working people naturally turn first to that which affects their daily life and they consequently combine first with their fellows by trade. It therefore becomes the duty of the members of the International to merely assist the members of the trade unions and, before all, to lead them to the right path, i.e., to internationalize them but also to establish new ones wherever possible. The economic conditions are driving the trade union with irresistible force from the economic to the political struggle against the propertied classes—a truth which is known to all those who serve the labor movement with open eyes." At this convention the Social Democratic Party was organized and it responded the following year to the invitation of the Knights of Labor to join in the labor conference at Pittsburgh. The socialists tried to capture the Pittsburgh conference for socialism, but their efforts only added to the factional difficulties within the ranks of the Knights. When the socialists tried to invade the labor movement by holding mass meetings among strikers, they found themselves in open conflict with the public. Their halls were raided, their meetings broken up, their speakers arrested, and their leaders driven out of cities where strikes were in progress.

A second attempt at political organization on a considerable scale was made at Newark in 1877 when the Socialist Labor party was formed. This party declared that the members should "maintain friendly relations with the trade unions and should promote their formation upon socialistic principles." It repudiated socialist military organizations and offered the ballot as the best weapon for the workingman. It was augmented in numbers in 1878, when a savage "anti-socialist law," passed by the German government, drove thousands of socialist refugees to America. It was this element and the trade union element in the United States that prevented the political radicalism of the National Greenback party from sweeping workingmen into the fold of the farmers' political organization. Nevertheless, the socialists soon fell out with trade unionism, pure and simple, and in time the Socialist Labor party denounced trade unionism of that type for its compromising tactics and its "political trading."

Socialists and the American Federation of Labor. —Notwithstanding the hostility of the Socialist Labor party, many socialists in the ranks of the American Federation of Labor continued their efforts to commit the Federation to socialist principles and independent political action. At each successive annual convention of the American Federation, Mr. Gompers stood his ground and held the Federation fast to the original doctrines. It is true that, from time to time, the Federation went on record as approving single propositions which were socialistic in nature, such as municipal ownership of utilities; but actions of this character are quite different from endorsing an independent political party of the working class and revolutionary changes in the capitalistic system of ownership and production.

The Socialist Labor party in national politics.— In 1892, the Socialist Labor party held a national convention in New York, nominated a candidate for president, and put forth a platform of principles, including government ownership of the means of transportation and communication, municipal ownership of utilities, progressive income and inheritance taxes, free school books, universal suffrage, the recall, and the referendum. This platform was moderate in tone and contained no reference to the revolutionary class struggle. The candidate in 1892 polled about 21,000 votes. The next presidential campaign, the Socialist Labor party became more radical in tone, declaring for the solidarity of labor, the class struggle against capitalism, and the collective ownership of the machinery of production. This time the vote was about 36,000. At each successive campaign the Socialist Labor party nominated candidates, issued a platform, and carried on an agitation though with diminishing party success. The vote of the party in 1916 was only 14,000.

The Socialist party.—Dissatisfaction with the leadership and tactics of the Socialist Labor party led to the formation in 1900 of a new socialist political organization, known at first by the name of the old Social Democratic party, and a year later as simply the Socialist party. The party in 1900 put forward as the candidate, Eugene V. Debs, the prominent leader in the Pullman strike six years before, who had been imprisoned for the violation of an injunction. It polled about 96,000 votes. This new Socialist party declared "the supreme issue in America to-day to be the contest of the working class and the capitalist class for the possession of the powers of government." It set forth a program of "immediate demands" such as government ownership of monopolies as well as mines, railways, etc. At each presidential election since 1900 the Socialist party has entered the campaign with a presidential candidate and a program. While the language of the platform varies from year to year, the spirit and purpose of the party have remained practically unchanged. The presidential vote rose to 901,000 in 1912, in spite of the radical program of the Progressive party; but it declined in 1916 to about 600,000.

Like all labor and radical parties, the Socialist party has been weakened by dissensions and splits. In 1905 a Socialist faction helped to form the Industrial Workers of the World. They were forced out of the party later owing to their advocacy of sabotage. A serious break came again in 1917 when the organization condemned the government of the United States for entering the war against Germany and avowed open hostility to the war program of the government. A number of prominent Socialists left the party and placed loyalty to their country above loyalty to the party. Several anti-war Socialists including the former candidate for President, Mr. Debs, were tried, convicted and imprisoned for their opposition to the war. The membership of the party declined. Although large votes were polled at local elections, as at Dayton, Ohio, and New York City in 1917, it appeared that the party as a political body had lost prestige and influence in national politics. Nevertheless, the ideas of municipal and government ownership remained as prominently before the public as ever.   Further inroads upon it were made in 1919 when the more radical "Left," impatient with the slow methods of political agitation and fired by the revolution in Russia, broke away from the Socialist party and founded the Communist party.   These new radicals issued a call for the overthrow of the capitalist system by labor and the establishment of the "dictatorship of the proletariat" as the beginning of the communist commonwealth.

4. THE ANARCHISTS

Definition.—Anarchy is a vague term.   There is but one thing on which the anarchists agree and that is hostility to the modern state or government.   They differ profoundly as to just what form of society they wish to substitute and how it is to be brought about.   They are at opposite poles from the socialists in that they reject the coercive authority of the state over the individual.   Such a control they hold to be fatal to the development of personal liberty, the right of a person to do as he pleases and develop his personality in his own way.   While socialists and anarchists are sometimes found together in opposing the policy of an existing government, they are at swords' points on all other questions. For the most part the anarchists dislike modern industrial society and see the hope of mankind in small communities combining agriculture and handicraft and governing themselves. In this they are reactionaries facing back to an old order destroyed by steam and machinery.

History of anarchism.—The history of anarchist theories runs back to ancient Greek days. Anarchistic books are found scattered all along through the centuries. The advocates of large individual freedom, like Herbert Spencer in England, verged over in that direction in so far as they viewed government interference with industry and socialistic tendencies as dangerous to life, liberty, and property. In the middle of the nineteenth century anarchy was given a great impulse by the writings of the French leader, Proudhon, who declared justice to be the supreme law, and the Golden Rule the guide to human relations. "I ought to respect my neighbor," he said, "and to make others respect him as myself." He rejected all government saying "the government of man by man is slavery." In three phrases he summed up his philosophy: "No more parties, no more authority, absolute liberty of man and citizen." From Proudhon's writings a whole school of anarchists developed. To his influence was added later the influence of two Russian writers: Bakunin and

Kropotkin. When Bakunin entered the labor movement he was able to split the congress of the International Workingmen's Association in 1872, carrying with him a large faction. Bakunin explained his position in this way: "We reject all legislation, all authority, all privileged, chartered, official, and legal influence—even if it were created by universal suffrage—in the conviction that such things can but redound always to the advantage of a ruling minority of exploiters and to the disadvantage of the most enslaved minority." He urged the use of armed violence in overthrowing the existing governments and the establishment of secret societies to spread the doctrine.

Kropotkin, though an enemy of centralized government and an advocate of violence, was unlike Bakunin in that he did not propose to establish "absolute individual liberty" but local communism. He proposed to form local coöperative and productive groups, living together under the control of "loving treatment, moral influence, and liberty." Kropotkin's celebrated countryman, Tolstoi, while embracing anarchistic doctrines, rejected all violence. He objected to the state because it was founded on force, and declared the supreme law of life should be the teachings of Christ, with love of mankind as the cornerstone. He advocated meeting force by passive resistance, and sought to exemplify his philosophy by living the life of a humble peasant, practicing the love and mercy which he preached. It was in Russia under the rule of the cruel and oppressive monarch, the Czar, that anarchy flourished like the green bay tree. The soil was well adapted to its growth.

Anarchism in America.—Persons holding theories tinged with anarchy appeared early in American history. Many of them went out on the frontier beyond the reach of the settlements and lived the life of the savage, without law and without government, practicing, if not preaching, anarchy. Others were theorists who looked upon government as an evil to be avoided as much as possible. This was but the logical conclusion of the doctrine: "the less government, the better." The "first American anarchist," as he is called, Josiah Warren, was prominent in the labor movement in the thirties and forties. He urged workingmen not to look to the government for help but to form "coöperative or communist colonies" on somewhat different lines from those advocated by Fourier and Robert Owen. In common with all the humanitarians of his time, he feared the state and thought that the way out of poverty could be found in private coöperative efforts of workingmen. The result would finally be, he thought, the disappearance of the government as a political instrument. Warren was followed by American thinkers of the same school, including John Campbell, Stephen Pearl Andrews, and Benjaman R. Tucker. They founded papers, wrote books and pamphlets, and carried on an extensive agitation on the fringe of the labor movement, appealing always for the support of members of the wage-earning class.

The Black International.—Anarchy entered into a new phase when, in 1881, the anarchists of Europe founded, in London, the International Working People's Association, known as the Black International. In October of that year an American branch was formed in Chicago with delegates from other cities, especially New York. The members declared themselves ready to "render armed resistance to encroachments upon the rights of the workingmen." They appealed particularly to those labor organizations that were arming themselves secretly against the troops, state and federal, employed in strikes. They endorsed trade union organization but rejected all political action. The most outstanding leader was a German anarchist, Johann Most, who had been expelled from the Socialist ranks and had suffered imprisonment in Germany and England for his anarchist activities. He advocated violence in the overthrow of church and state and "his ideal society was an agglomeration of loosely federated autonomous groups of producers." Each group was to follow its own trade and own the means of production. There was to be no superior over the group and exchange was to be carried on through the medium of paper money. Just how conflicts among the groups were to be avoided or settled was not clearly set forth.

This vague philosophy, strong in denunciation of the existing order, made headway especially in Chicago where even the Central Labor Union gave aid and support and marched in the processions of the Black International. As long as the anarchists were mainly foreigners and few in number and confined their activities principally to discussions of their theories, little attention was paid to them. When, however, in 1885 a great demonstration of the unemployed was organized by the anarchist leaders and the English-speaking workingmen took part in the proceeding the public was aroused. The Chicago. *Arbeiter-Zeitung* exultantly exclaimed: "Yesterday the typically American working-class carried the red flag through the streets and thereby proclaimed its solidarity with the international proletariat." The next year occurred a serious labor disturbance in connection with a strike. Working-men were raided by the police, without warrant, they claimed. Subsequently a huge mass meeting of workingmen was held in Haymarket Square, and the police in full force arrived upon the scene. Some one threw a bomb which killed a sergeant instantly and wounded many others. Thereupon the police fired upon the crowd.

The whole city was thrown into a panic by this affair. The press called for the immediate and

merciless extermination of the anarchists. Several
Internationalists were arrested. Four of them were
hanged; one committed suicide; and three were condemned to prison where they remained until par-
doned in 1893 by Governor Altgeld. It was not
proved at the trial that any of these men threw the
bomb or were actually implicated in the bomb throwing; but it was shown that they entertained and
preached extreme doctrines, and urged violent resistance in case of collisions with the police.

American public opinion was deeply stirred over
the throwing of the bomb and the trial, especially
because seven of the eight men arrested were aliens.
The labor world was stirred also. The Knights of
Labor refused to ask for clemency for one of the
accused who had been a Knight for many years.
They took the ground that the public might construe
such action as implying sympathy with violent
methods. The American Federation of Labor, on
the other hand, did ask for clemency for all the
condemned men, while repudiating violent methods
in strong terms. Thoroughly frightened by the outcome of the Chicago disaster and heartily condemned
by public opinion and organized labor, the Black
International speedily lost its hold. Another anarchist organization, the Red International (so
called from the red cards of membership) which had
been running parallel with the Black International,
was able to continue its operation mainly because it

was opposed to violence and advocated a long campaign of peaceful agitation to prepare workingmen for the day of revolution.

The effect of the Haymarket riot upon the organized labor movement is hard to gauge. If statistics of membership may be taken as a measure, the slow growth of the American Federation of Labor for years after this affair and the dissolution of the Knights of Labor would seem to indicate that anarchistic affiliation had retarded the advance of the regular labor and craft organization. Nevertheless, there has always been an anarchist group attempting to attach itself to organized labor and influence its counsels.

5. THE INDUSTRIAL WORKERS OF THE WORLD

Since the seventies, there has been in the American labor movement a strong group of leaders who have opposed the organization of the working class into separate crafts or trade unions, and have advocated the formation of one grand union embracing all workers as equal and alike in their interests. A number of purely industrial unions were early formed on this basis, and the Knights of Labor represented a very vigorous effort in this direction. The idea was never lost to sight in the labor ranks and reappeared in 1905 in the organization at Chicago of the Industrial Workers of the World. This organization was a merger of (1) the Western Labor Union, formed in 1898 through the efforts of the Western Federation of Miners and called in 1902 the American Labor Union; (2) the Socialist Labor party; (3) and other radical groups of smaller importance. All these organizations had been hostile to the American Federation of Labor, first because it was exclusive, being confined to the more skilled workers; secondly, because it accepted the capitalist system and the trade agreement as final; and thirdly, because its scheme of organization and its tactics were objectionable to the radical "industrial democrats."

The program and methods of the new organization.—The Industrial Workers really introduced no ideas or tactics that were new in the world. They were an evidence of the tenacity of old labor theories and the persistence of revolutionary organizers. While they theoretically accepted the socialist doctrine of the social production of wealth managed through a collectivist state, they believed that the idea was too complex for a simple working person to grasp. They were, moreover, uneasy about the growth of state socialism fostered by the middle classes. They feared that the poorest paid and unorganized workingman might suffer quite as much under the coercive authority of a government conducting industries as under private owners.

Their idea was to organize all the workers in each

of the great industries into one big industrial union and to weld the organizations so formed into one national industrial organization. Their collectivist proposal was that each industry was to be managed by those employed in it and each local unit by those employed in that. They did not oppose the idea of government, but distinctly declared that there must be government in the shop, the school and "in the conduct of the public services." They treated wage bargains and the closed shop with contempt, regarding the best of bargains as mere concessions which labor had to make in its extremity. While approving the use of the ballot to gain possession of the existing government they declared that the great revolution was to come through the action of the workers in their several shops and industries in seizing the plants, tools, and materials with which they worked. Being, many of them, migratory laborers, they could not always vote themselves.

They argued that the division of laborers into crafts, drawing closer and closer with employers in interlocking contracts, tended to weld the skilled workmen and the capitalists into one class opposed to the masses of unorganized workers. They saw in the craft union something monopolistic, the craft limiting apprenticeship and resisting all improvements in production that change the old methods. They saw in the internecine warfare going on among the crafts a source of pleasure and strength to the employers. They declared labor to be broken into bits and the capitalists to be taking advantage of the situation. Therefore they began to work for solidarity. They took up the cry of the Knights of Labor, "An injury to one is the concern of all," and the socialist slogan, "Each for all and all for each."

In order to arouse the interest and coöperation of the very poorest workers, the Industrial Workers fixed the initiation fees and dues at a low figure. They gave large autonomy to the local unit. They trusted to the quick and effective strike because their funds would not permit the prolonged battles that the well financed trades unions could wage. In case of the failure of the strike and the return of the workmen at the old wage or worse, they advocated *sabotage,* that is, the stoppage of machinery or some other interference with the industry so as to check production. In short, their tactics were to win concessions by short strikes and penalize employers if they lost by curtailing profits as far as possible. Sabotage was not new when the Industrial Workers took it up. It had been practiced by the Knights in the railway strike of 1885, but it was brought prominently to the attention of the world as an instrument in labor warfare by the action of the French unionists, or syndicalists, early in the twentieth century.

Strikes of the Industrial Workers.—The year following its organization, the Industrial Workers entered a strike at Goldfield, Nevada, where a contest between conservatives and radicals in the labor camp, similar to the old battle between the Knights and the American Federation, was going on. In 1907 the western miners withdrew from the Industrial Workers, depriving them of their strongest financial and moral support. The next year the brewery workers, also a powerful union, split off. In 1908 the Socialist Labor Party element withdrew and set itself up as a separate I. W. W. group.

These defections were partly offset in 1912 by a great strike in Lawrence, Massachusetts, where the textile workers struck in a body and waged a spectacular battle against the employers. A Congressional investigation revealed the distressing conditions that prevailed in a large section of the textile industry, and the spirited agitation of the radical labor leaders brought the membership of the Industrial Workers up to 30,000. Later strikes at Paterson, New Jersey, for example, were less successful and it was clear that the organization could not make rapid headway in membership and strength against the more conservative American Federation of Labor. The strike was long and funds were low.

During the War against Germany the Industrial Workers collided with the government on a number of occasions. Their leader, William D. Haywood, and several other members of the organization were indicted and imprisoned under the Espionage act.

Federal and state laws were enacted providing penalties for acts of sabotage. The Industrial Workers of the World was put in the class of "outlawed" organizations. California was especially severe on it: by the terms of an injunction issued in that state it became a crime to advocate that the workers take over industry and the government. The courts in general held that mere membership in the organization was sufficient cause for arrest and officers of the law applied it without mercy.

In spite of its legal outlawry and its disfavor with the trade unions, the organization in 1924 had 37,600 dues-paying members. Its strength lay mainly among the migratory harvesters and lumber men of the Far West whose economic life and problems were peculiar, presenting one of the most baffling of all the labor issues in America.

CHAPTER XII

LABOR AND THE WORLD WAR

Contrast with the position of labor in the Civil War.—During the Civil War there was no such thing as a committee to control labor standards for war clothing, equal pay for equal work without sex discrimination, government wage scales regularly made in consultation with labor organizations, or labor representation on war boards. As we have seen, labor organization itself at that time was too demoralized and weak to exercise much influence on the course of events. The Civil War, however, stimulated organization so that labor was stronger at the close of the struggle than at its beginning. The progress made by labor in organization and power since the sixties is well illustrated by its changed position during the World War.

The effect of the war on industry.—As in the case of the Civil War, the European conflict gave a great impetus to American industry. The demand for manufactured commodities as well as foodstuffs became enormous; the demand for labor increased accordingly. European immigration was practically stopped; prices rose; labor called for higher and higher wages to meet the rising costs of living and got them; and the trade unions grew rapidly in membership and the number of locals. As before, prosperity contributed to the advancement and strength of organized labor.

"This is labor's war."—The American Federation of Labor accepted the war as its own democratic struggle. The Executive Committee issued the definite statement in February, 1918, that "this is labor's war." Knowing that from three to twenty industrial workers were essential for the equipment of every soldier in the field, Mr. Gompers, at the first sign of American participation in the war, took steps to guarantee that equipment. At a conference of workers summoned by him on March 12, 1917, at which the Railway Brotherhoods were represented as well as the Federation of Labor, organized labor accepted the war whole-heartedly and only asked for certain stipulations in return for its effective co-operation; namely, trade-union working standards in war work, equal pay for equal work so that standards of living might not be lowered by the inevitable drafting of women into industry in war time; and the representation of labor on war boards. Pro-war socialists joined with trade unionists in the summer of 1917 to form the American Alliance for Labor and Democracy.

Members of the unions who were pacifists strenuously objected to labor's acceptance of the war idea. They felt that labor's industrial position was imperiled by its attitude and they formed that same summer the Workmen's Council for the Maintenance of Labor's Rights. Its life was ineffective and brief.

Labor in the war government.—The loyal stand of Mr. Gompers and the American Federation of Labor was immediately appreciated. The necessity of avoiding disturbances in the war industries, coupled with the knowledge of the strength of organized labor, led the government to accept, in the main, the labor stipulations, especially about labor representation in the war administration. Mr. Gompers was at once placed on the Advisory Committee of seven to help the Council of National Defense as chairman in charge of labor relations. In that capacity he was largely instrumental in preventing the relaxation of labor laws during the war. Only four states broke down their labor legislation and only one of these, Massachusetts, enforced the modifications.

Eventually organized labor was represented on the coal, fuel, food committees, on the war industries and emergency construction boards, and, of even more significance, on the treasury committee on the taxation of war profits.

The chief labor administrator as an important Cabinet member.—Labor as a real factor in the shaping of policies was still more clearly seen with the rise of the Secretary of Labor, W. B. Wilson, a former miner, to a position of positive influence in the Cabinet. Two boards were organized largely on his initiative to perform the duties of labor administration. First of these was the National War Labor Board created in April, 1918, to adjust disputes between employers and employees. Some 1500 cases came before this board for adjudication and in general its awards were accepted. The second of these, the War Labor Policies Board created in June, 1918, was charged with laying down the principles to govern the relations between capital and labor in all the adjustments made during the war. These principles dealt with collective bargaining and protective standards of health and safety.

Both capital and labor being represented on these boards a truce was virtually declared to the effect that output was not to be limited by strikes or lockouts and both sides were to sacrifice in the matter of wages and profits. Collective bargaining was accepted with an arbitration instead of a strike provision and established safeguards for health were to be maintained. The eight-hour day was to be continued where it existed by statute and applied as widely elsewhere as necessities for supplies and the health of workers would permit in the opinion of high federal authority. A living wage for all workers, skilled and unskilled, was called for. Standards governing the work of women acting as substitutes for men were also fixed to include the eight-hour day, one day of rest in seven, prohibition of night work and of industrial home work, equal pay and health protection. Women advisers representing organized women workers and social workers were drawn into the war administration to formulate and watch over the application of these principles.

The Department of Labor became one of the war centers of the nation. It numbered among its duties the insuring of a labor supply, the protection of labor interests, the collection of facts and their dissemination, industrial housing, transportation, the standardization of working conditions and wages, and the establishment of uniform labor clauses in all government contracts. Owing to the number of agencies controlling labor finally brought under the jurisdiction of the Department, labor was said to be "in the saddle."

A feminist problem.—Women who replaced men worked mainly in machine shops such as munition plants, automobile factories and repair shops. In January, 1918, the most authoritative estimate placed the number of women making war supplies at 1,266,000. They were also used extensively on steam and electric railroads in a variety of ways.

One of the most interesting phases of the new industrial position of women developed in the street railway service in Cleveland toward the end of the war. A definite feminist movement appeared there. The women, on the one hand, declared their inherent right to choose their own occupations in face of grand jury declarations that the street cars were no place for women. On the other hand, the transit employees' unions showed a decided reluctance to admit women as members, preferring to shut them out of the service altogether. Suffragist sympathizers with the women and the National Women's Trade Union League stood for the right of the women to keep their employment though they recognized that the conditions of that employment could be improved. The federal War Labor Board overruled the feminists and the male trade unionists carried the day.

Labor disturbances during the war.—In spite of labor's official acceptance of the war as its own and its share in labor administration with its manifold machinery for watchfulness and adjustment, all was not smooth sailing in the prosecution of the war. According to the report of the American Federation of Labor there were 1515 strikes in 1918 involving 234,466 workers and costing $1,474,380.79. Large as was this number of strikes it was claimed that it was below the normal rate. It is also recorded that 203,876 of the strikers materially improved their conditions of labor.

Among the disputes seriously affecting war industries was a very brief strike called by the Railway Brotherhoods shortly before the declaration of war in March, 1917, as a protest against delays in applying the Adamson eight-hour law. The immediate yielding of the railway managers through government pressure prevented the stoppage of the railway service. To facilitate the transportation of troops and supplies the government took over the administration of the railroads in December of that year. Government management of the telegraph and express services soon followed.

The strike called by the International Union of Mine, Mill and Smelter Workers, one of the Federation of Labor organizations, in Bisbee, Arizona, led to a local civil war which aroused the whole country. The mob spirit developed among citizens who charged the striking miners with pro-Germanism and revolutionary intent fostered by Industrial Workers of the World agitators. Miners and their sympathizers were deported by citizens, who took the law into their own hands. It was not until federal troops fed, guarded and returned the deported strikers to their homes that quiet was restored and the authority of the government recognized. As a result of a government investigation, several leading citizens were indicted.

In the lumber regions of Washington and Oregon, where material for airplanes was secured, for one thing, an outbreak resembling the Bisbee trouble occurred in July and August, 1917. This time it was the Industrial Workers of the World who called the strike and their demand was for an eight-hour day. Eventually the lumber operators conceded the demand, but not until the federal troops were again used, and much bitterness created in all circles. The general lawlessness that such labor disputes aroused, and the hysteria that provoked lynchings and murders, called forth a protest from President Wilson against the mob spirit. That unfortunately did not end all the race rioting and anti-alien demonstrations, most of which had their basis in strife between capital and labor.

Labor at home affected by labor abroad.—The course of events in Europe during the war exercised a marked influence on the development of labor opinion in the United States. The Russian Revolution and the establishment of a government professing to represent only the working class fired the imagination of the radically inclined workers in this country. The subsequent Revolution in Germany and the election of a socialist saddle-maker to the presidency of the new republic, though in fact conservative as compared with the overturn in Russia, was watched with keen interest by the labor movement in America. Perhaps of a still greater significance to American trade unionists was the formation of a British Labor Party of "hand and brain workers" with a state socialist program which it explained as an attempt to build a new social order.

Mr. Gompers and the pro-war Socialists realized

full well the interaction of labor unrest and propaganda. Through the Alliance for Labor and Democracy they continually tried to hold organized labor to the main issue of the war. They interpreted the war again and again to labor at home. They went abroad to explain to foreign workers the loyal position of American labor with a view to preventing labor in the allied countries from swinging to pacifism and "Bolshevism," thus weakening the prosecution of the war.

Mr. Gompers' labor dream.—Mr. Gompers looked ahead in "labor's war of democracy against autocracy" to a magnificent consummation in the peace settlement: the industry and loyalty of labor had contributed largely to the outcome of the war and now this invaluable contribution to democracy was to be recognized clearly and internationally. At the Peace Conference in 1919, Mr. Gompers was made president of the international commission on labor legislation and he exerted a marked influence on the course of events. At this time labor received a forward-looking charter of freedom binding on all the signatory nations. This charter was to be developed through a League of Nations in which labor representatives, holding the same intimate and effective position which they had enjoyed in their own governments during the war, would have world power.

Recognition of labor in the Peace Treaty.—Recommendations were presented to the Peace Conference by labor organizations in various countries. American organized labor felt that it was influential in helping to secure the nine specific clauses in the treaty. These labor clauses granted to employees the right to organize for all lawful purposes; a wage in harmony with a reasonable standard of living according to the time and country; an eight-hour day; one day's rest in seven; abolition of child labor; equal pay for equal work of men and women. A draft convention also incorporated in the treaty, provided for a permanent organization to promote the international regulation of labor conditions.

The preamble of the draft convention is of deep significance because it shows the first world recognition of labor movements and labor claims. It reads:

WHEREAS, The League of Nations has for its objects the establishment of universal peace, and such a peace can be established only if it is based upon social justice; and

WHEREAS, conditions of labor exist involving such injustice, hardship and privation to large numbers of people as to produce unrest so great that the peace and harmony of the world are imperiled; and an improvement of these conditions is urgently required; as, for example, by the regulation of the hours of work, including the establishment of a maximum working day and week, the regulation of the labor supply, the prevention of unemployment, the provision of an adequate living wage, the protection of the worker against sickness, disease and injury arising out of his employment, the protection of children, young persons and women, provision for old age and injury, protection of the interests of workers when employed in countries other than their own, recognition of the principle of freedom of association, the organization of technical and vocational education and other measures;

WHEREAS, Also, the failure of any nation to adopt humane conditions of labor is an obstacle in the way of other nations which desire to improve the conditions in their own countries.

The International Labor Conference.—The first international labor conference held in accordance with the terms of the treaty assembled in Washington in October, 1919. Considerable friction developed in the conference because the governmental and official representatives predominated over the bona fide labor men. The representatives from the Central powers were admitted to membership, notwithstanding strong opposition from some delegates. The conference laid out a program to be recommended to the League of Nations. The chief features of it were the eight-hour day, the forty-eight hour week, government provision for the unemployed, the limitation of the labor of women and children and provision for the education of children employed in industries.

The Women's International Labor Conference.— Women were not directly represented at the labor conference in spite of their requests for representation. The National Women's Trade Union League, on the suggestion of British and French working women, called an International Working Women's Conference which met in Washington simultaneously with the men's conference. There were no governmental representatives at the women's conference naturally. Nor was the conference recognized by the American Federation of Labor. Delegates were present from Great Britain, France, Italy, Norway, Sweden, Japan, Argentina, Czecho-Slovakia, Poland and Canada, as well as the United States. Resolutions were sent to the men's conference calling for international protective legislation for mothers, a forty-four hour week, better provisions against unemployment, prohibition of night work for women and for men except in case of essential public service, and the raising of the age of working children to sixteen. Protective legislation for women had long been one of the main purposes of the National Women's Trade Union League, whose activities centered mainly on the eight-hour day, the minimum wage, health insurance and abolition of night work for women. It added to these, following the rush of women into federal service, a demand for equal opportunity and pay in the Civil Service. The International Working Women's Conference had the immediate effect of encouraging the economic organization of women in this country and arousing their political enthusiasm. It also spurred those who opposed restrictive legislation for women to greater propaganda for "Equal Opportunity."

The Pan-American Labor Conference.—The strained relations that existed between the United States and Mexico on the outbreak of the war led the American Federation of Labor to take steps to bind the labor movements of the two countries closer together. After a visit to Mexico by an American labor mission, a permanent Pan-American Labor Federation was formed in November, 1918. Impetus toward this movement was given also by the fact that the Pan-American Union had no labor representation in its councils. Five years previously the American Federation had voted against intervention in Mexico and had congratulated the Mexicans on their "war for freedom." It now organized to promote more friendly relations.

Reconstruction program of the American Federation of Labor.—Although they were accustomed to periods of reaction after periods of labor advance, leaders were amazed at the suddenness of the movement toward wage reductions which set in with the signing of the armistice. An emphatic protest was immediately issued calling attention again to the part labor had played in the war and the necessity for equal standards for labor in peace times.

To make those gains permanent the American

Federation drew up a reconstruction program as did other labor and civic associations in this country. The program was sanctioned by the annual convention at Atlantic City in the summer of 1919. A summary of that program follows:

Responsibility of the government for legislation to prevent child labor exploitation;

The participation of the people in coöperative agencies for food and commodities distribution;

Federal and state regulation of corporations including the increasing of capital stock and bonded indebtedness;

Democracy in industry whereby the employers' interference with the right of workers to organize should be made a criminal offense and workers should have a voice within industry and commerce similar to their political participation;

Government ownership and operation of docks and wharves;

The development of state colleges and universities for educational opportunities for all people;

The joint supervision of trade unionists and employers in federal, state and municipal employment agencies;

No employment agencies to be operated for profit;

Maintenance of free speech and assembly;

Public and semi-public utilities to be owned, operated or regulated by the government in the interest of the public;

Government supervision and aid for housing facilities and home building;

Immigration restriction and regulation;

Regulation of land ownership;

Legislation, reënacted by Congress or state legislatures after having been declared unconstitutional by the Supreme Court, to become law;

Government control of the merchant marine to protect rights of seamen;

Opposition to militarism;

Democratic organization and control of militia;

Non-partisan political policy for labor;

Right of public employees to collective bargaining;

Employment and land allotment for discharged soldiers;

Tax upon incomes, inheritances and land values;

Right of teachers to organize and affiliate with the American Federation of Labor;

Opposition to the doctrinaire economists' position on the causes and remedies for unemployment;

The wage question, as the fundamental economic and social question;

Federal and state ownership and operation of water ways and water power;

Equal pay for equal work;

State insurance to supplant employers' liability insurance operated for profit.

Organized Labor and the "Reds."—In the autumn of the same year (1919) the officers of the Federation made an attack on the Communists and other radicals in the labor movement, disclaiming on the part of organized labor any sympathy with revolutionary theories or activities. It fell to the lot of the Secretary of Labor, through his subordinate, the

Commissioner of Immigration, to enforce the act of 1918, excluding and expelling from the United States all anarchists and persons calling for the violent overthrow of the existing order. The provisions of this Act were not limited to the war emergency. At the end of the year the first shipload of deported persons was sent to Europe and hundreds of other radicals were "rounded up" for deportation.

Politics again at work—the American Labor Party.—As a result of European influence and domestic factors like the high cost of living, the renewed battle with the courts growing out of the use of injunctions in the miners' strike, the failure of the steel strike in 1919-20, free-speech interfer- ence and other forces, signs of another political uprising appeared within the American labor move- ment at the close of the Great War. The American Federation of Labor at its annual convention in 1919, it is true, declared its adherence to the tra- ditional policy of opposition to independent political action. Nevertheless local organizations affiliated with it, especially in New York and Chicago, broke away from the leadership of the Federation on this point, and formed independent local labor parties. The central federated unions of both these cities went over in a body and officially to independent political action. The success in the municipal elections of 1919 was not particularly encouraging to the sponsors of the movement but they called a national convention of trade unionists in Chicago in November of that year and launched a national American Labor Party.

The Convention was composed of about 1,000 delegates representing labor organizations in thirty-seven states and the District of Columbia. A striking feature was the presence of women, not yet nationally enfranchised, but confidently expecting the ratification of the federal suffrage amendment which came the following summer in time for the presidential campaign. The nomination of a candidate for president and a platform were deferred but a declaration of principles was announced.

The purpose of this new party as stated in its Constitution was the "union of hand and brain" workers for "political, social and industrial democracy." Membership was not to be confined to unionists alone nor to wage earners alone. The Constitution provided for a National Committee made up of two delegates from each state, one of whom was to be a woman; for a referendum to members on campaign issues; against the nomination of candidates on tickets of the old parties; for the expulsion of any member accepting the nomination of another party; and for working alliances if possible with "farmers' leagues and other progressive organizations supporting the Labor Party's program and accepting its ideals."

The platform, drawn at a second convention, in
1920, consisted of thirty planks, representing a com-
posite of sweeping Socialist doctrines, progressive
legacies from the Bull Moose party, and trade union
reforms approved at annual conventions.   These
planks included demands for the repeal of the Espionage act; free speech and assemblage; a League
of Nations built on the "fourteen points"; nationalization of "all basic industries which require large
scale production and are in reality upon a non-
competitive basis," like mines and forests; the Plumb
railway plan—a scheme backed by the Railway
Brotherhoods for government ownership of railways
with participation of employes in the management;
steeply graduated income and inheritance taxes;
government management of the banking business; a
national executive budget; abolition of the Senate;
nationalization of unused land; abolition or curtailment of the right of the Supreme Court to veto legislation; popular election of federal judges; credit
facilities for farmers "as cheap and available as those
afforded any other legitimate and responsible industry"; guarantee of the right of collective bargaining;
prohibition of child labor under sixteen; and a wage
"based upon the cost of living and the right to maintain a family in health and comfort without labor of
mothers and children."

Several important farmers' organizations were active in this convention, writing their demands into

the platform and adding another link in the history of farmer-labor alliances in America. All in all the effort represented a wide movement for a public political appeal with a radical program. It was not only the railway men who were pressing for the government ownership of a great utility. Miners, too, well represented by delegates to this convention were demanding the nationalization of the mines; first the Western Miners voted for it and then the United Mine Workers at their 1919 meeting in Cleveland.

The strength of this independent political organization encouraged another drive on the American Federation of Labor to make it change its rigid policy of abstention from third party movements. Furthermore the new insistence that the worker must be lifted from the status of a mere wage-earner to that of participation in the management and profits of industry brought the wages policy of the Federation again into review. But its wages theory had been moving to new ground anyway as a result of war experiences. In 1918 the Executive Council of the Federation, declaring that "we are each day building Labor's house of to-morrow," had called for labor participation in industrial management and a determination of wages with relation to increasing power of production instead of the cost-of-living—the older and narrower basis.

While radicals were preparing for an independent
contest at the polls and the Federation was shaping
up its own program, capitalist forces were making a
drive on radicalism that alarmed all classes of labor.
Drastic peace time seditions bills were threatened by
Congress early in 1920 and Mr. Gompers expressed
the fear that these might be applied to conservative
unionists after the "Reds" had been disposed of.
With his old vigor he led the Executive Council of
the Federation, therefore, in a program to capture
state legislatures and Congress in the approaching
November elections.   This victory was not to be
achieved by a departure from the established non-
partisan policy of the Federation, but by the aggressive application of that policy.   The Federation was
to "reward friends and punish enemies," on the
theory that the 4,000,000 labor votes in the country
would constitute a balance of power for which the
old parties must bid high.   Wherever it was possible
to place a labor representative on the ticket of the
old parties that method was to be used.

The aggressive political policy of the Federation
seemed to encourage rather than to intimidate the
young American Labor party.   Its confident chairman in New York declared: "There must be political
organization to carry out the political program of
the American Federation of Labor and there must
be a political organization to support it after election.
Labor is sick and tired of relying on the pre-election

promises of political decoys of men controlled by the old machines, of men elected by campaign funds contributed by the corporations. . . . The more attention the American Federation of Labor gives to politics the better. The more active participation by the Federation promotes education in politics, and it leads inevitably to the conclusion in the minds of the unionists that a labor party is necessary, and in endorsing labor representatives the Federation will have to come sooner or later to the one party which alone can furnish labor representatives."

The Presidential Campaign of 1920.—The advocates of independent political action for labor determined to put their cause to a test in the campaign of 1920. A second convention at Chicago chose the name of Farmer-Labor party and nominated Parley Christensen of Salt Lake City, and Max S. Hayes, of Cleveland. The new party was endorsed by six international unions, seven state federations of labor, and hundreds of city central labor bodies. It had presidential electors on the ballots of seventeen states. In the agrarian northwest, co-operation with the Non-Partisan farmers' movement was effected with striking results. In the election which ensued local achievements ran ahead of the national showing. Municipal and congressional campaigns yielded a number of victories but the national candidates polled only about 275,000 votes out of a total of more than twenty-six millions. The Socialist vote was more than three times the size of the Farmer-Labor vote. Mr. Gompers threw his support to James M. Cox, the Democratic candidate, who fell about seven millions short of the vote polled by Warren G. Harding, the Republican victor. An analysis of the vote in the working class districts of the great cities in that election shows conclusively that the varied appeals made to those who toil evoked varied responses when they cast their ballots. The third and last conference of the Farmer-Labor party was held in 1923.

CHAPTER XIII

RECENT LABOR DEVELOPMENTS

International affairs.—The American labor movement followed with close and intense interest the results of the war in Europe. Serious conflicts developed within its ranks under the influence of events abroad. Supporters of the Soviet Republic of Russia pressed their communist principles upon American workers by means of straight propaganda, educational organization, boring within the Federation of Labor, and efforts at distinct communist party organization. Even the communists themselves, following the course of events in Russia, split into a left and a right wing with many intermediate factions. Mr. Gompers and the Federation, however, adhered without faltering to their established policy of accepting the capitalist system and bargaining with it. They vigorously attacked every proposal to have the Soviet Republic recognized by the government of the United States.

Nevertheless they did not adhere to the doctrine of isolation in international affairs, even though the American Senate refused to ratify the Treaty of Versailles, for the League of Nations covenant with its labor program was an integral part of it. In the

172

international conferences that were called to establish and develop the provisions of the labor pact, the representatives of the American Federation of Labor were present as keen observers. Of necessity their influence was unofficial—a strange incident in view of the fact that Mr. Gompers had been one of the framers of the labor sections of the Treaty. While thus working on the side lines, Mr. Gompers and the Federation continued to support the League of Nations in principle and to argue for the constitutional and coöperative, instead of the revolutionary, method of gaining power. They argued in this vein at the International Conference of Trade Unions held at Amsterdam in 1919 where strong pressure was exerted in the opposite direction. They maintained that position at home.

In Latin-American relations, the Federation has been a definite peace maker and partial shaper of Mexican labor history. Viewing the de la Huerta rebellion as an anti-trade union movement, with all that that implies, Mr. Gompers used every resource of the Federation to win American support for the Obregon régime. Undoubtedly its influence was a material element in the forces which led the American government to open direct negotiations with Mexico, recognize the Obregon government, and establish formal relations in March, 1924. In all Pan-American affairs the Federation has thrown its support on the side of friendly relations. Repre-

sentatives of the Federation were sent to study
conditions in those islands of the Caribbean Sea
where charges were made against our government by
the workers. On their return the representatives
placed before the Federation certain proposals for
the reform of administration in the islands, including an announcement by our government of the date
of its withdrawal from Santo Domingo.

National policies and legislation.—A striking
departure from American traditions was made in
1919 when the United Mine Workers declared in
favor of the government ownership of coal mines.
In 1922, a miners' strike brought the coal industry
to such a crisis that the federal government barely
escaped the necessity of assuming control of the
mines. It appointed a Coal Commission which
studied the situation and severely criticised the
whole industry, reporting in minute detail the evils
it discovered and their relation to the life and labor
of the miners and their families. The Commission
did not endorse the proposal of the United Mine
Workers but it did declare the coal industry to be
"affected with a public interest" and therefore a
proper subject for strict government control. In its
conclusions, the Coal Commission approached the
Federation of Labor's position, so often stated by
Mr. Gompers; namely, that an economic order of
self-governing industries is better than the socializa-
tion of industries. It urged federal coöperation

with the coal industry and coöperation, within the industry itself, among its three essential elements— operators, miners and dealers.

The question of government ownership versus the alliance of labor and capital in a system of self-governing industries has constantly cropped up in the labor movement since the war. In 1920, the Federation of Labor declared for government ownership and democratic control of railways according to the Plumb Plan. The declaration of a policy was relatively simple. It was not so simple for responsible officials to carry it out. Two years later a severe and prolonged strike of railway shopmen broke the continuity and efficiency of the service. All kinds of proposals were advanced by the public for the suppression of the strike and the prevention of such disturbances in the future. In these circumstances, the Executive Council of the Federation of Labor gave its support to a measure finally introduced in Congress in 1924 to provide "means by which the management and employees through representatives of their own choosing shall confer on the problems of the 'human side' of railroading." It was hoped that through such conferences collective agreements could be reached respecting wages and working conditions and all the other matters in controversy. Confidence in the ability of the industry to clear up its own troubles was reiterated. The government was urged to keep its hands off. Twenty-one railroad organizations approved this proposed measure which, if enacted into law, would repeal the labor clauses in the Esch-Cummins Act—the source of such bitter strife between capital and labor.

There was still another way in which the issue of government ownership of great utilities came before the labor movement. In 1923-4 there was rather suddenly revealed to the American mind the limitless possibilities for increased production that lay in the extension of "giant power" throughout the country. The term "giant-power" is applied to hydro-electric power generated at places like Niagara Falls, Great Falls (Montana), and at the Muscle Shoals and Columbia River developments and transmitted to distant regions by wire. The term is also applied to the power generated from coal directly at the mines and transmitted by wire for hundreds of miles. Prophets of a new age foretold the coming of a single network of power transmission across the entire continent. Actual organization in six or more adjoining Eastern states for the development of giant power from coal and water seemed to be, in 1924, the next important link in the cross country chain.

Now mechanical power in production is the most striking American industrial fact. It makes the distinction between poverty and labor in this country and poverty and labor in countries where the muscle of men and women is the basis of production. Naturally, therefore, with the prophecy of a tremendous growth in mechanical power within the next few years in America, the labor movement faced the issue of the ownership and administration of that power. Whom is giant power to benefit? The situation was clearly stated by Mr. Gompers: "We as a people shall be foolish indeed if this tremendous development is allowed to roll its great weight upon us without any action on our part looking toward its control and direction. We have before us an opportunity to take one great engine and compel its course so that it shall be to the largest possible extent a well balanced social asset, instead of an engine run primarily for profit and only secondarily for service. . . . Surely human intelligence is capable of something better than the railroad muddle in the development of power. Surely it is capable of something better than the muddling of the mining industry." His own solution for the impending problem was the same solution upon which he insisted for the railroad and mining muddles: namely, to avoid "blighting political domination" by instituting the "orderly process of democratic management" in the development and transmission of giant power, with "full and public industrial accounting." The question of ownership he declared was not paramount; the question of administration was the leading issue.

Thus the executives in the American Federation of Labor steered as far away as they could from the radical agitation for the government ownership of public utilities. "Industry's Manifest Duty" was declared to lie in the direction of ending the conflict between industrial groups. In a printed appeal, widely distributed by them, this duty was pressed upon the workers:

"The end of such a state of affairs must come at no distant time, or political bureaucracy will gain the ascendancy. And we cannot do other than regard such an eventuality as the final mark of incompetency to manage an industrial civilization. Industry must save itself. Industry must find itself. Industry must organize for service, for constructive effort, for orderly continuity, for justice to all who participate. It must bring itself to a realization of its mission and to that end it must organize and come together in deliberative bodies where the full wisdom and experience of all may contribute to final decisions. Much the same lessons that we have learned in our political life—among them the sense of order —must be learned and given effect in our industrial life. Fact must take the place of opinion and selfish interest. To function must be the object and democratic participation of all who give service must be the mechanism that makes this possible. Industry must realize that it exists to give service to a nation and not to a single master, or to a syndicate of stockholders. We must have an American industrial life, an American industrial order, not a warring group of units, each seeking to be a law unto itself, the

while inviting the interference of those whose compe-
tence is at best an unknown factor."

The future society sketched by Mr. Gompers was
a sort of guild society with farmers and capitalists in
the picture. When, however, he was drawn into debate and his books were brought under review, he was
asked a number of trenchant questions. Is there
such a thing as "the public" to be considered in any
particular case, such as a dispute between miners
and mine owners? If so, has that public any rights
which the disputants are bound to respect? What
agency other than the state can enforce such rights?
When all industries are organized on self-governing
principles, what agency other than the state can medi-
ate among them? If a special agency is created, how
will it differ from the existing state? Who is to
adjust conflicts among industries? Who is to prevent the powerful and essential industries from ex-
ploiting the weaker and less essential groups?
Should the owners of forests and the lumber workers
be permitted to cut the forests of America all down
and sell the lumber to foreign countries without let
or hindrance? Should the building trades be permitted to check or control an educational program?
Since taxes fall on production, who is to determine
the nature and incidence of the taxes laid for the
support of education and other public services?
When the discussion passed from the realm of general principles to that of action, no one was quicker

than Mr. Gompers to recognize the significance of
the state and to make use of it in securing positive
gains for labor. Indeed the history of the Federation on one side is the story of its activities in support of constructive political measures.

While the Federation has been debating the larger
industrial issues it has been pushing its immediate
program of national legislation with greater vigor
and by means of an increased legislative lobby.
Pressure upon Congress is now exerted by the Trade
Union Legislative Conference Committee consisting
of between thirty and forty persons representing the
great international unions and the railroad brotherhoods. The 1923 report stated that in the Sixty-
seventh Congress as many as 400 bills affecting labor
were introduced and that, out of these, the Federation secured the passage of 12 favorable laws, defeated 16 unfavorable laws, and lost 5 which were
unfavorable but passed in spite of the opposition of
the Committee. Among the measures which the
Committee supported was the proposed amendment
to the federal constitution permitting Congress to
enact child labor legislation—an amendment made
necessary after the Supreme Court had declared two
successive child labor laws unconstitutional. Among
the measures which the Committee opposed was the
bill giving the federal courts jurisdiction over the
enforcement of treaty rights of aliens; they declared
that it could be used to defend non-union labor and

make the federal government a "giant strike-breaking agency." The Committee also opposed the bill providing for the deportation of aliens who take part in "riotous gatherings" on the ground that it would give the federal courts jurisdiction over all workmen's meetings. The abolition of the Railroad Labor Board, created by the Esch-Cummins Act of 1920, was demanded on the ground that it favored the railroads at the expense of the employees and was an "unwarranted political invasion of the field of wage-fixing and employment relations."

Labor and the courts.—While organized labor has been instrumental recently in defeating many bills in Congress, it has itself suffered a number of defeats in contests with the judiciary. In fact, under repeated decisions, the labor clauses of the Clayton Act have been utterly riddled. During the strike of the railroad shopmen, in 1922, the federal Attorney-General, Harry M. Daugherty, secured from the district court of Chicago an injunction against the strikers which is one of the most sweeping decrees ever issued in a labor dispute. The injunction was sustained on appeal. Under this decree, union leaders were forbidden not only to picket, but also to issue any statement or to order the members of their organizations to leave their work or persuade others to do so. Miners, printers, machinists, the men's clothing workers, and other labor groups have all had their days in court since the war. As decisions of the Supreme Court now stand, unions are not exempt from the law when they commit an "unlawful" act; the injunction may be issued whenever any material damage is being done to an employer; trade unionists cannot agitate among non-union employees who have an agreement with their employer for the maintenance of an open shop; only that kind of picketing is lawful which is carried on by individual unionists stationed at or near plants; trade union leaders and agitators from the outside cannot lawfully interfere in a controversy between an employer and his workers; the secondary boycott is illegal; and a trade union may be sued under the Sherman Act for damages done to an employer in a strike.

Political unrest and its expression.—As in former times, when the injunction was used against labor and resentment took the form of political action, so again many leaders turned to the ballot in their quest for a remedy. Labor's activity in the congressional elections of 1922 led to the defeat of several candidates of the Republican party for the House of Representatives. Contests were waged throughout the country. In that stronghold of iron and steel interests, Jefferson County, Alabama, five active labor leaders were sent to the state legislature. Labor blocs appeared in local and national bodies.

As the 1924 elections approached, radicals again worked for a wider, more united, more "progressive," and more militant political campaign. The injunction was but one plank that figured in the program of the next independent political movement, born in Cleveland early in July, 1924, at the Conference for Progressive Political Action. The Railway Organizations were the chief backers of this Conference. The nature of their occupation and its close relation to government and law made political action especially vital to them. With the paper, *Labor,* the educational agency for this group had been established in 1919. But the Conference was also supported by other strong labor unions and indeed its chairman was William H. Johnston, President of the International Association of Machinists. Groups of farmers, socialists, and progressives in general were represented.

When Senator Robert M. La Follette and Senator Burton K. Wheeler accepted the nomination as the candidates of the Conference and endorsements began to come in from the outside, it seemed that this new political movement represented the most formidable array of interests yet mustered for a radical campaign. Farmers' organizations in great numbers affiliated, because they were pleased with the program for agricultural reforms. The Socialist party joined officially and Morris Hillquit, one of its ablest spokesmen, was put on the central committee. And the crowning achievement was the final endorsement by the Executive

Council of the Federation of Labor itself. Mr. Gompers and the other officials took this drastic step after the Republican and Democratic parties refused to incorporate the labor proposals into their plat-forms. The Executive Council stated most emphatically, however, that, in endorsing the candidates they were not giving their approval to a third party movement. On the contrary it was with consistent adherence to the Federation non-partisan policy of "punishing enemies and rewarding friends" that they turned to senatorial friends and a friendly platform. Senator La Follette's labor record was extraordinary; it could not be ignored. The hopes for a labor vote *en bloc* rose high. And as quickly died away when Wisconsin alone was carried.

The evolution of collective bargaining. (1) Federal employees. —While it debates and tries political action, organized labor wins from time to time important economic-political victories. For example, the postal and other government services have been forced to adopt more enlightened employment policies since the civil servants have triumphed in their long struggle for the right to form unions. By an act passed in 1912, Congress reversed President Roosevelt's executive order which had forbidden federal employees to press demands for higher wages and better conditions of employment. During the World War organization was made very difficult by the hostility of Postmaster-General Burleson and

other government officials to the unionization of
the government service. But with the end of the
war the next great step was taken toward the
elimination of the spoils system in the government
service. Labor organizations throughout the government service now present their proposals for reform
in a manner that is declared to "represent the growing spirit of the dignity of the service, of a corporate
life centered in the service of the nation, a changing
attitude toward the service of the state." In this
new development of collective bargaining, post office
clerks took the lead. Then letter carriers, railway
mail clerks, and finally rural mail carriers formed
associations and received charters from the American Federation of Labor. The National Federation
of Federal Employees, in its charter of affiliation
with the trade union movement, acknowledges its special obligation to the public and does not proclaim its
right to strike and tie up the public service. It has
worked for the improvement of the service. It
secured from Congress in 1923 a Reclassification
Bill which instructed government agencies to introduce standards of labor and reward in the place of
inefficiency and favoritism. The politicians cannot
dispose of "political plums" so easily now.

(2) The Glenwood experiment.—In one great public service under private management there has also
been a marked advance in collective bargaining. Following the railroad shopmen's strike in 1922, the

Baltimore and Ohio Railroad consented to try an experiment in coöperation between the management and the employees which was so successful that the plan has now been extended to the forty-four branches of the Baltimore and Ohio Railroad and to the Canadian national railroad. The experiment was made in the repair shop at Glenwood, in the Pittsburgh district, starting in February, 1923. Though one of the three major repair shops for the Baltimore and Ohio Railroad, the Glenwood plant had hitherto been the first to shut down and the last to reopen in a crisis. Hitherto also shop committees had been mere "purveyors of grievances." Collective bargaining had been confined to struggles over hours and wages; the spirit of the men was low; production was correspondingly low. The new plan gave the shop committees a chance to function in a larger way; it gave them a voice in the actual management of the shop. Tools were improved, supplies put on a better basis, production was stabilized, costs were reduced and plans were drawn up for the creation of repair reserves for periods of depression together with budgets and other measures for the prevention of crises. The men responded enthusiastically to the larger opportunities and responsibilities and when the first locomotive to be built under the new scheme, Engine No. 1003, left the shed, the whole plant viewed her as the symbol of a new order.

The success of the Baltimore and Ohio experiment is largely due to the fact that the labor organizations involved were fortunate enough to secure the services of an engineering technician of wide experience and large social sympathies to guide the scheme. In this evolution of collective bargaining therefore there are those who see a deep social significance, a new spirit dawning in American social relations. They look forward to an increasing alliance between the engineering technician and the labor movement. They see the trend toward the desire of the expert to serve society in such a way that the "dream of coöperation between the managers of industries and their labor forces" will materialize "in an economically sound reality." Studies recently made by a research bureau seem to indicate that more permanent results come when the coöperation takes place between voluntary labor organizations which are a part of the regular trade union movement than when the coöperation is between management and company unions.

(3) **Stabilizing industry.**—The trend of the labor movement as a whole is unquestionably toward increased influence in the stabilization of industry. This is evident in the steady lengthening of trades hitherto purely seasonal; in the reduction of unemployment with its devastating social effects; in attempts to break the historical rhythm of prosperity and depression; in the checking of an over-supply of

labor by means of drastic immigration legislation, thus giving to workers already employed a high purchasing power in the market; and in the growth of a serious study of management problems. The strike is slowly, but surely, yielding to the trade agreement as employers recognize the strength and persistence of the union movement; labor welcomes the chance to deal with employers in the more amicable fashion. A strong impetus was given to the search for solutions of management problems by President Harding's Conference on Unemployment with its subsequent reports dealing with seasonal operation, business cycles and depressions, and similar matters. In the development of the two official reports, labor participated, making substantial contributions; and the reports have in turn been used by labor executives to advantage. The International Ladies Garment Workers and the Amalgamated Clothing Workers have secured the first assumption of joint responsibility by industry and labor for unemployment insurance, a device more constructive than benefit funds which simply mitigate the hardships of unemployment.

Labor research.—Organized labor early recognized the importance of collecting industrial statistics and other data bearing on labor questions. It was instrumental in securing the establishment of the bureau of labor in the Department of the Interior in 1884 and continued its agitation for greater support and appreciation of this service until it saw the organization of the separate Department of Labor in 1913. During the World War that Department made valuable contributions to the maintenance of industrial harmony but since the War it has required constant vigilance on the part of labor to prevent the crippling of the Department by inadequate and discriminatory appropriations.

The need for careful and minute studies of the leading industries is being brought home more and more to the workers. In controversies over hours, wages, and other matters, a union is in a much stronger position when it has definite knowledge about the conditions of production, capital, profits, dividends, markets, and other factors in the case. For the assumption of any responsibility in any industry, such facts are basic. But it is not easy to determine the best method of making scientific surveys. In some instances, unions have employed professional experts, statisticians, lawyers, and economists to make the special studies; in other instances, they have resorted to research bureaus outside the ranks of labor but in sympathy with the movement. No matter what agency is used, the problem of getting specialists with the true scientific spirit is always present. Nevertheless, organized labor recognizes that it cannot wage its battles without using the weapons forged by a correct and technical knowledge of all the elements involved. It is therefore discussing in its conventions the best means of "centralizing, analyzing, and disseminating information in connection with industrial conditions and problems."

Financing the labor movement.—The entrance of the trade unions into the field of banking is an after-the-war development in which labor takes great pride. The reasons for undertaking the organization of banks are thus advanced in a set of resolutions presented to the national convention of the Federation in 1920:

WHEREAS, There are no banking and credit agencies in the United States controlled and operated in the interest of the worker and the farmer, to which these groups can go for cheap and easy credit, in emergency, in sickness and in need; and to which they can apply for credit to develop their talent and initiative; and

WHEREAS, The wages of labor and the wealth of the farmers constitute a great part, possibly two-thirds, of the credit resources of America, which wages and agricultural wealth are often used by the banks against labor, against the farmer, against the producing classes; and

WHEREAS, Practically every other country in the world has banks and credit agencies owned and operated by the workers in their own interest; and

WHEREAS, Such banks have increased the power of organized labor, have given it a sense of solidarity and resourcefulness, and have improved the standard of life of the people; now therefore be it

Resolved . . . that the American Federation of

Labor urge the enactment of laws by the nation and by the individual states that will permit of the organization of coöperative or people's banks. . . .

Resolved, That organized labor mobilize its money, its deposits and its resources and use them for increasing the economic power and the solidarity of labor.

By 1923 some twenty-three banks were doing business or were ready to begin and about twenty more were being organized. The success of the banks led the Executive Council of the American Federation of Labor to study the whole problem of banking and to consider the formation of a federation or central bank at Washington. The Committee reported its findings to the convention of 1923:

We have pointed out the ideal of credit administration through a public agency. We feel constrained to point out that no appreciable progress toward that end has been recorded but we cannot but feel gratified at the great interest aroused by our analysis and our proposal. Through the growing number of labor banks some progress toward the ideal may be made. Most progress consists of a compromise between conditions and the ideal. Labor banks are much nearer to the masses of the people than are the institutions of what is commonly called Wall Street; and they are more responsive to fundamental needs. As banks we look upon these institutions as helpful, even though they constitute no remedy. They may force remedies for some of the more glaringly inexcusable exploitations of the banking and financial world. If, through the development of relations between labor banks on sound lines, there can come into being a credit administration in the interests of productive effort, in the interests of true human progress, in the interests of service to society, we shall have reason to look upon labor banking as having the character of a truly fundamental step in advance. If there is hope to be seen in the development of labor banking institutions we feel that it must be through the development of a great agency for the constructive administration of credit.

The woman-in-industry question.—While labor's long battle with the courts against the injunction leads it into political organization, a new form of legal contest leads it into more intensive economic organization. In 1923 the United States Supreme Court declared the Minimum Wage law for women in the District of Columbia unconstitutional and this decision placed in jeopardy the minimum wage laws of twelve states, affecting one million five hundred thousand women. It did even more. It endangered the whole body of protective legislation for women built up through the years in state after state. Labor had been strongest among the forces that had secured such laws and it had supported them with the object of safeguarding the millions of working women outside the trade union membership. Suddenly, without warning, that prop against exploitation was menaced and the woman-in-industry question rose to the rank of a main issue in the organized labor movement.

Woman labor leaders led the debate on the issue. Enfranchized since the war, they felt a new sense of power. They reviewed the history of the American Federation of Labor and its affiliated unions in their attitude toward working women. They charged the movement with failure to take working women seriously, with unwillingness to face the fact that women are in industry to stay, with closing its ranks to women in some cases and in others with working but half-heartedly for the organization and incorporation of women into the unions. They pointed out once more that the position of women in industry has a vital relation to men who are trying to improve standards of living, especially while the competing women remain outside the unions. Owing to the pressure for a more vigorous policy toward women workers, a special conference was called of national and international unions having women in their industries. When it met in Washington in February, 1924, more aggressive action was determined upon and a committee was designated to work out a program. The plans that finally emerged provided for the supervision and direction of the activity by the president and executive council of the Federation. The work itself was to be carried on by an organizing council made up of representatives of the unions affected, acting with an executive secretary appointed by the president of the Federation from the union ranks and given an office in the Federation headquarters. To the secretary was also given the task of preparing educational and informational matter on women and industry. Each union was asked to state what financial and organizing support it would give to the program. In spite of the grave difficulties attendant upon the organization of women, it was hoped that results might thus accrue from central management of the campaign, coöperation with locals, and the pooling of funds.

Increasing solidarity of all workers.—While efforts to draw working women more closely into the labor movement were being made, the economic solidarity of workers was being strengthened in other directions also. Race as well as sex came under review after the war. Obviously colored workers were in industry to stay. By a few unions they had been accepted as members; from others they were excluded. In 1920, organized labor took a definite step toward the elimination of the color line in industry by providing for the incorporation of negro workers into all the unions and for the financing of negro organizers to push the unionization of their fellow workers. Organized labor went still further in its efforts to eliminate the color line by supporting equal privileges of citizenship, "regardless of race, creed or color." It recognized the service rendered by the negro soldier in the World War, "who fought

for the freedom that is due every human being," and
it declared that it had never countenanced the drawing of a color line in the matter of the suffrage. Organized labor also went on record against the persecution of people of other races and creeds by the
Ku Klux Klan.

Solidarity of labor was thus strengthened by the
efforts to reach out to the more helpless workers. It
was strengthened also by the voluntary accession to
its ranks of professional workers, such as teachers,
actors, technical and semi-technical experts. After
the war, hospitals complained of the scarcity of
nurses and the cause was largely attributed to the
low pay and lack of humane conditions for the nurses.
The same cause was assigned for the scarcity of
teachers and their rapid withdrawal from the profession. The commercialization of the theater had
reduced public entertainers to a master-and-servant
status and actors of high rank joined the poorly paid
subordinates in union activity to increase the dignity
of the profession. To all these new types of unionists affiliating with it, the American Federation of
Labor offered political, as well as economic, assistance, in case of need.

Workers education.—As we have seen above
(pages 39-43), organized labor had great influence
nearly a century ago on the establishment of the
public school system in the United States. From
that time forward, it stood firmly for the generous

support of free education. In its early agitation,
however, it was thinking mainly of equal opportunity for the children of the workers to rise from
the ranks of manual toil into the employing class or
into the professions. In recent years, other ideas
have been taking form. The Rand School, founded
in New York City in 1906, was based upon a new
concept; the school was conducted by Socialists for
socialist ends. In general, the present aims of labor
leaders, with regard to workers education, center
around the idea of making it of service in immediate struggles and in some ultimate social program.
Credit for initiating adult education under trade
union control belongs to the International Ladies'
Garment Workers' Union which established its Workers' University in New York City in 1916. Years
of devoted effort have now been given to this work
by the Educational Department of that Union and
much of the original apathy, opposition, and indif-
ference on the part of the rank and file of the membership have been overcome. The increased leisure
which its members enjoy as a result of the Union's
activities has thus been utilized by far-sighted leaders for training in history, economics, social institutions, and the liberal arts. Interest in workers education under trade union auspices grew rapidly
throughout the country. Within five years there
were fifteen labor colleges with an enrolment of ten
thousand students. Some of the regular universities

opened extension courses for workers. Soon there was a resident school, Brookwood College, at Katonah, New York.

Since 1921, the official educational work among trade unions has been under the supervision of the Workers Education Bureau which has offices in New York City and in the Federation of Labor Building in Washington, D. C. Several leading unionists are on its executive committee. In 1924 the unions voted a per capita tax on their membership for its partial support. The fifth year after its organization nearly 500 national and international unions, state federations, central and local unions were affiliated with the Bureau while the students enrolled in classes throughout the country numbered more than 40,000. In order that concise and inexpensive treatises on important subjects might be made available for students, the "Workers Bookshelf" was organized and rapidly extended. Education committees, field secretaries, summer schools and Labor Chautauquas were among the features of labor's awakening to the need of wider reading and discussion of economic and social questions.

Those engaged in this work realize that they should not expect quick results or an impressive statistical showing; that it is a matter of digging a deep foundation patiently and with a purpose that is invulnerable to discouragement. It was so in the beginning with the Workers' Education Association in England, which was partly responsible for the peaceful revolution that gave Great Britain a Labor Government in 1924.   It would be difficult to attach too much significance to the following testimony from the Labor Prime Minister given at that time: "Whoever moves about and spends frequent evenings as I do at the firesides of workmen, sees the result of this (workers' education), not only in the splendid collection of books which these families frequently possess, but in the intelligent level of conversation maintained and enjoyed at those firesides.   One does not find the decadent modern novel there nor the two-penny-half-penny monthly magazine, nor the picture daily paper.   One has to go to 'better society' for those.   However surprising it may seem to those who have no intimate contact with these circles, I assert with the greatest confidence that their intellectual level is higher than that of many learned university coteries and incomparably higher than that of wealthy manufacturers' families; better reading matter goes into those homes and the range of their interests is wider."

In view of the battles that rage around the matter of general public school education in this country, it is small wonder that adult workers education opens up a new battle ground for contesting theorists, interested factions with various ends in view, pure

idealists, conservatives, well-wishers, and even enemies of labor.

Those who are most active in the education movement, at present operating through the Workers
Education Bureau, are seeking to follow this general
plan: (1) a curriculum that is not a mere channel of
propaganda but a means of acquiring greater knowledge and larger truth through a wide range of
studies; (2) freedom from outside economic pressure
and excessive inside political control; (3) the tutorial
method of instruction with abundant freedom of discussion; (4) the largest possible exercise of democratic control by the students over the methods and
the choice of teachers.

Immigration has enormously complicated the
problems of workers education in America. Thousands of laborers are totally illiterate. Thousands
more know no English and must concentrate upon a
study of the language for a considerable time. Furthermore the educational movement is growing at a
time when aggressive educational insurgents are
found on every hand. Among the left wing groups
are the Trade Union Educational League—a national
organization with local branches; the Proletariat University of Michigan; the Proletarian Party, the Communist Party and the Workers' Party. The radicals
dwell upon the necessity of shaping education along
class lines. The Federation officially emphasizes the

fact that, while workers' education may start as a class movement, ultimately it will, like all other labor activities, find a wider expression.

At the convention of the Federation in 1923, the Secretary of the Workers Education Bureau made this broad appeal:

We believe it advisable at this time to consider certain well-defined tendencies which the labor movement must take into account in its educational program. Maintenance of democratic ideals and sustained progress of a democratic nation are possible only with constantly broadening standards of education. There never was a time when the problems of life were more intricate or more momentous. In world politics we seem to be at the cross-roads—in event of orderly progress we can proceed toward the development of world institutions through which to conduct international affairs and make possible such progress in the industrial arts and intellectual and social culture as even our dreams cannot forecast and the alternative road leads to chaos and the waste and futility of continuous war. In national affairs there is in the making the development of fundamental principles to underlie group activity as well as the technical basis for increasingly effective endeavor. The fabric of our social structure is so interwoven that activity is interdependent and by groups instead of individuals separately. In this complexity of social tissue, the decision of any industrial issue becomes of far-reaching significance, affecting the welfare of many different elements in industry and society.

It is therefore tremendously important that labor

make only well-based decisions on all issues, and this can be done only with broad and accurate sources of information, for labor holds constructive and decisive relationship to the fundamental problems of living. Experiences of the past in recorded form should be made available for the work of each succeeding day. In addition we must have much more of general knowledge and a more penetrating understanding of the philosophy of life to enable us to discern surely those things which are of permanent value.

Death of Samuel Gompers.—The American Federation of Labor owes its inception and achievements largely to Samuel Gompers. In the capacity of president and chief spokesman for organized labor, he served the Federation for forty-two years. At the age of seventy-four, his death came in a peculiarly dramatic manner—while he was demonstrating to Mexican workers his sympathy with their cause and his desire for mutual understanding between the two countries. He had gone to Mexico City from El Paso in 1924, with a large delegation from the American labor convention to attend the convention of the Pan-American Federation of Labor and be present at the inauguration of Plutarco Calles as labor president of Mexico. He was not well at the time and this strain was too great at his age. Rushed back to the border, he died on December 13 at San Antonio. The burial was at Tarrytown, New York.

Gompers left to his successor the presidency of a great estate built up by decades of tireless endeavor.

This consisted of a stable and efficient national organization; a great volume of labor legislation; a working scheme for educating the rank and file of the membership; and a program for domestic and foreign procedure which had withstood the batteries of radical fire for forty years. Attacks on the rising standard of American living by European immigrants had been materially reduced and Oriental labor shut off. Friendly relations had been established with labor throughout the western hemisphere and efforts to extend the idea of arbitration by support of the League of Nations and World Court had been made. It was a giant machine which Gompers and his counsellors bequeathed to the next directorate—a machine with a mind operating, American fashion, in such fields as banking, credit, insurance, investments, and economic research. Its notion of its manifest destiny was running close to that of the nation.

The New President, William Green.—From the largest union in the Federation, the United Mine Workers, came the successor to Mr. Gompers. William Green was no novice either in the economic or political field when he assumed this office. He had been secretary-treasurer of his union and third vice-president of the Federation. Besides his long affiliation with organized labor, he had served in the Ohio Senate where he drafted the workmen's compensation law of the state and on three occasions he was a deledate to the national Democratic convention. He understands the American institutions which Mr. Gompers begged his successors to cherish well.

INDEX

203